Also by Michael J. Gelb
Published by Delacorte Press

HOW TO THINK LIKE LEONARDO DA VINCI

THE "HOW TO THINK LIKE
LEONARDO DA VINCI" WORKBOOK

DA VINCI

DECODED

Discovering the Spiritual Secrets of
Leonardo's Seven Principles

MICHAEL J. GELB

DELACORTE PRESS

DA VINCI DECODED
A Delacorte Press Book / October 2004

Published by
Bantam Dell
A Division of Random House, Inc.
New York, New York

Book design by Ellen Cipriano

The terms *High Performance Learning, How to Think Like Leonardo da Vinci* and *Curiosità, Dimostrazione, Sensazione, Sfumato, Arte/Scienza, Corporalità,* and *Connessione* are trademarks of Michael Gelb. All rights reserved.

This book presents information which may or may not be right for you. In view of the complex, individual, and specific nature of health and healing issues, this book is not intended to replace professional advice. Every individual is different. The publisher and the author expressly disclaim any responsibility for any loss or risk incurred as a consequence of the application of the contents of this book.

Library of Congress Cataloging in Publication Data

Gelb, Michael.
Da Vinci decoded : discovering the spiritual secrets of Leonardo's seven principles / Michael J. Gelb.
p.   cm.
Includes bibliographical references.
ISBN 0-385-33861-9
1. Creative thinking.   2. Leonardo, da Vinci, 1452–1519.   I. Title.

BF408.G364 2004
158.1—dc22
2004052717

Manufactured in the United States of America
Published simultaneously in Canada

10 9 8 7 6 5 4 3 2 1
BVG

To the timeless, universal spirit of
Leonardo da Vinci

May God, light of all things,
deign to enlighten me, who here treat of light.

—LEONARDO DA VINCI

CONTENTS

INTRODUCTION: THE UNIVERSAL MAN

There is a light within a person of light,
and it shines on the whole world.

—THE GOSPEL OF THOMAS

Perhaps you saw the episode of *Star Trek: Voyager* in 1997 when Leonardo da Vinci debuted as the holographic adviser to the captain. Leonardo's sage advice was instrumental in guiding the ship and crew to fulfill their highest purpose, to boldly go where they'd never been before. In the following pages, I'm hoping that you'll discover Leonardo as your personal spiritual adviser, a guide who can help you to discover and fulfill your highest purpose—just as he has helped me.

I also hope you'll find inspiration from many of the other voices in this book, each of whom may be able to add to your understanding of your own life purpose. Not long ago at a conference in Venice to which we had both been invited, the renowned physicist Michio Kaku gave a speech that put a new spin on my concept of what a meaningful life would be. Dr. Kaku—who, as it happens, served as one of the scientific advisers to the writers of

Star Trek—is the cofounder of string field theory, author of such international best-sellers as *Hyperspace, Visions,* and *Beyond Einstein,* and the Henry Semat Professor of Theoretical Physics at the City University of New York. Speaking before an audience of company presidents at that 2001 conference, Kaku enchanted those down-to-earth, no-nonsense executives with his theories about the existence of life on other planets. Not only does the best scientific thinking support the idea that there is such life, he explained, but it is likely that in the vastness of the universe there are civilizations that have evolved far beyond us. Unfortunately, he said, we are at the lowest level of civilization, insofar as we are in danger of destroying our environment and each other.

The next tier up, what Kaku calls Level One (our own tier not even meriting a number), are civilizations that have ensured their own survival by advancing their technology and consciousness to the point that they can feed, clothe, and educate all their members while protecting and nurturing their atmosphere and ecosystem.

The highest tier, Level Two, are those civilizations that have aligned themselves with pure consciousness and are able to travel through time and space powered solely by clarity of intention (like Q in *Star Trek*). Emphatic about the fact that this isn't science fiction but rather the best assessment of many of our greatest scientific minds, Kaku suggested that we on planet Earth have a window of less than one hundred years in which we can evolve to Level One—or else sink into the oblivion of self-destruction.

The core message of this speech resonated deeply with me. For whether we take Kaku literally or metaphorically, his story offers a powerful way of thinking about our destiny and focusing our attention on the bigger picture of our life's purpose: help the earth get to Level One! This we can do only if each of us makes a personal commitment to the process of conscious evolution.

In his acclaimed *New York Times* best-seller *The Seat of the Soul,* Gary Zukav offers a guide to the kind of heightened consciousness that will get us to that next level, which he describes as the "territory of inspiration," the place where intuition accelerates, putting us in touch with something beyond ourselves, something beyond "the realm of time and space and matter . . . something of great vision that comes from beyond the personality." As he believes, "Each of us is now being drawn, in one way or another, to that same great vision. It is more than a vision. It is an emerging force. It is the next step in our evolutionary journey."

Zukav describes this evolutionarily more advanced consciousness as being more open to intuition, to subtleties in awareness and the promptings of the soul, because it is "multisensory," in contrast to the usual "five-sensory" mode of experience, which is oriented only to physical reality and personal survival.

According to Zukav, the five-sensory human operates as though:

+ Each of us is alone in a vast, empty, purely physical universe.
+ Our power of intention is ineffectual, and our actions have only their immediately apparent physical effects.
+ The physical environment must be dominated to ensure survival.

The multisensory human operates as though:

+ The universe is a living expression of divine intelligence, and we are all part of something much greater than our own ego / survival.
+ Our intentions are powerful determinants of our reality and have a profound effect on others.
+ Our world is designed for us to learn and serve our soul's true purpose.

Leonardo is an early but uniquely advanced embodiment of the kind of multisensory awareness Zukav describes. With his endless curiosity, his openness to all kinds of experiences, his gift for seeing God's intelligence in everything in the world around him, Leonardo provides us with a compelling map for the "territory of inspiration." If we look to him for inspiration in our own lives, he can guide us in taking our next evolutionary step—as the greatest souls always do.

As Zukav says, "With each of our individual advancements, the group soul of humanity—what we call our collective unconscious—evolves." No one in all of human history made "individual advancements" more extraordinary than Leonardo da Vinci. It is fitting that his influence is greater now than ever before. Still, it is surprising to realize how ubiquitous a figure he has become in recent years.

Although Leonardo's greatness might seem to be something almost supernatural, his accomplishments reflect his very human openness to intuition and inspiration—qualities that we can learn to incorporate into our own lives. As an avatar of multisensory awareness, Leonardo is a prophet of the divine potential inside every being. He can point all of us toward the path to our higher selves.

Indeed, every major spiritual tradition encourages the study of exemplars of the path. Hindus seek to emulate the apparent perfection of great teachers such as Ramana Maharshi or Ramakrishna. Christians ask, "What would Jesus do?" And Buddhists reflect, "How would the Buddha respond?" Recently, a number of books have cast light on the relevance of divine teaching in worldly contexts—for example, a manual for CEOs based on the teachings of Jesus, and a guide for singles inspired by the Buddha. This kind of contemplation helps us integrate great wisdom into our daily lives.

Unfortunately, models and images of wisdom, goodness, love, and beauty aren't easy to come by in popular culture and the mass media. Imagine watching the news and following the stream at the bottom of your screen as it moves along: "Leonardo's lost notebooks recovered . . . but first, more on the latest celebrity scandal." As a society, our priorities for the investment of attention are frequently out of alignment with our highest ideals.

There's actually a neurological explanation for this. One of the paradoxes and challenges of the human mind is that we are conditioned by the brain's reticular formation (a structure in the midbrain) to pay special attention to anything that seems new, different, or "sensational," while allowing more timeless, less topical material—such as universal spiritual wisdom—to be forgotten. But matters of the spirit always eventually resurface precisely because they are timeless and universal, as we can see from the fact that all of the diverse societies of the globe, at some point in their development, have arrived at fundamental insights that are remarkably similar. Author Aldous Huxley called it "the perennial philosophy." One research group found that at least eight of the ten commandments are common to all the world's cultures, constituting the equivalent of a global statement of human values. As my secretary, the venerable Mary Hogan, puts it: "We may root for different teams, but we all love baseball."

In the course of my spiritual search I've been fortunate to learn from many great teachers from different traditions. I've been blessed with *darshan* from gurus of pure lineage and experienced the searing brilliance of J. Krishnamurti's spiritual razor. I spent months learning meditation with the guidance of the abbot of a Cambodian Buddhist monastery, and I traveled to Turkey to dance with the dervishes and receive initiation from a Sufi sheikh. I was gifted with the opportunity to listen and learn every day for ten months as J. G. Bennett, the remarkable spiritual genius, shared the fruits of his lifetime of seeking. I've received Holy Communion in an ancient English church alive with spirit, and I've offered supplication while facing Mecca with my brothers who follow the teachings of the prophet Muhammad. And, of course, I was called to the Torah at thirteen and am bar mitzvah.

No teacher, however, has influenced me more than Leonardo. When I wrote my first book about him, *How to Think Like Leonardo da Vinci*, I discovered seven principles underlying his life and work that seemed to explain his creativity and point the way to ours. The same seven principles also seem to explain

THE LEONARDO WAVE

About five hundred years before you picked up this book Leonardo da Vinci was putting the finishing touches on the *Mona Lisa*. Over the centuries since his lifetime—he was born on April 15, 1452, and died on May 2, 1519—he has been the subject of wave after wave of scholarly attention and popular fascination. Sometimes the speculation, mystery, and controversy that continue to surround his life and legend cause those waves to crest. But in the last ten years the waves have been swept into a veritable tsunami of excitement. Here are just a few of the peaks:

1994: Bill Gates pays $30.8 million for eighteen pages of Leonardo's notebooks.

1995–1996: Ten-volume comic book, *Chiaroscuro: The Private Lives of Leonardo da Vinci*, published in the Vertigo line of DC Comics.

1996: Shawn Colvin album *A Few Small Repairs* released; includes a song entitled "You and the *Mona Lisa*."

1997: On a *Star Trek: Voyager* episode, John Rhys-Davies guest-stars as a holographic Leonardo, helping Captain Janeway overcome several nasty obstacles.

1998: In *Ever After*, a Cinderella movie starring Drew Barrymore, Leonardo da Vinci, rather than a fairy godmother, assists the protagonist.

1998: *How to Think like Leonardo da Vinci* is released and appears on several best-seller lists.

1999: Spectacular restoration of Leonardo's *Last Supper* completed after twenty-two years of meticulous labor.

1999: Twenty-four-foot-tall bronze *Leonardo Horse*, envisioned by Charles Dent and executed by Nina Akamu, is unveiled in Milan (exactly five hundred years to the day that the original clay model was destroyed by invading French troops). Its twin is dedicated at the Frederik Meijer Gardens and Sculpture Park in Grand Rapids, Michigan, as a tribute to Leonardo's spirit.

2001: Artist Vebjørn Sand's exquisite Leonardo Bridge linking Norway and Sweden is dedicated by Queen Sonja of Norway. Sand proposes a plan to build a Leonardo Bridge on every continent as a symbol of our love of beauty and our links to one another.

2002: Italian one-euro coin appears with the figure from Leonardo's *Vitruvian Man* on the back.

2002–2003: Metropolitan Museum of Art in New York City sponsors unprecedented and wildly popular exhibition of Leonardo's drawings.

2003: Mary Zimmerman's play *The Notebooks of Leonardo da Vinci* packs the house at New York's Second Stage Theater.

2003: Leonardo goes Hollywood again: *How to Think like Leonardo da Vinci* is featured in the opening scene of *The Italian Job*.

2003: Dan Brown's *The Da Vinci Code* debuts and proceeds to smash all sales records for a novel.

2004: Oxford University Press releases Professor Martin Kemp's superb *Leonardo: A Very Short Introduction*.

2005: The Da Vinci Center of Science and Technology opens in Allentown, Pennsylvania.

2006: "The Universal Leonardo," a simultaneous global exhibition celebrating Leonardo's genius, coordinated by Professor Martin Kemp, begins.

Leonardo's Bridge is an inspiring symbol of universal love and connection.

the source of the spirituality that emanates from all his work—inventions, paintings, scientific experiments, and writings alike. That quintessentially spiritual quality is what makes Leonardo the ideal of the *uomo universale*, the Universal Man, someone who can speak to the longings all of us share. And if there is anything I've learned in my travels during the last twenty-five years in Australia, Japan, Turkey, Europe, Scandinavia, Latin America, Africa, and the United States, it is how much we do share.

The meetings I've been fortunate enough to have with remarkable teachers from the world's diverse wisdom traditions have only reinforced this perception of our essential unity, as it is expressed in our common spiritual inheritance. There are many paths to the top of the mountain, but there is only one summit—love.

The challenge is to make us see universal wisdom in a new light, to capture the attention of the brain's novelty-sensitive reticular formation with examples that have enough freshness and originality to remind us of what we all know but often forget. Who better to personify universal wisdom and make it come alive for us than Leonardo? His life is a colorful, vivid archetype of human potential, and his works yield something new each time we look at them. But what is best about both the life and the works is their timelessness. Leonardo's soaring spiritual greatness brings to mind the strengths that are at the heart of all faiths, from Christianity to Judaism, Islam, Hinduism, Buddhism, and Taoism. Like all those who have attained true wisdom, Leonardo gives voice to values and ideals that are universal, a core body of truths that unite rather than divide us.

Hailing the Benefits of
"Walking with the Wise"

Judaism teaches: "He who walks with wise men shall
be wise, but the companion of fools will suffer harm."
(*Proverbs*)

The Hindu tradition reminds us: "In the company of
the wise even fools may attain to wisdom."
(*Mahabharata*)

And Buddhism counsels, "One should follow
the good and the wise, as the moon follows
the path of the stars."
(*Dhammapada*)

Sufi master Hazrat Inayat Khan illuminates the search for universal wisdom in this entreaty: "Allow us to recognize Thee in all Thy holy names and forms: as Rama, as Krishna, as Shiva, as Buddha. Let us know Thee as Abraham, as Solomon, as Zarathustra, as Jesus, as Muhammad, and in many other names and forms, known and unknown to the world."

I feel incredibly lucky and deeply blessed to have the opportunity to share this exploration of the spiritual application of Leonardo's principles with you. It is a project that makes my heart smile. I've also discovered that writing directly about spirituality is extremely humbling. As Guru Arjan Dev, of the Sikh tradition, notes: "Were the earth to become paper, the forest pens, and the wind a writer, the end of the Endless One could not be described." And the Sufi mystical poet Jalaluddin Rumi sings: "When I try to describe Thee my pen breaks and the paper slips away."

Each of us must find our own path, our own relationship to the Divine, and come to terms with our life's meaning and purpose. My wish is that the contemplation of the spiritual meaning underlying Leonardo's principles may help to point the way.

OVERVIEW: POINTING THE WAY

Fix your course to a star.

—LEONARDO DA VINCI

The purpose of this book is to provide practical guidance and inspiration for your personal growth and spiritual journey based on the inspiring wisdom of history's greatest genius. I'll show you how Leonardo's seven principles reflect universal spiritual insights and how you can integrate those insights to bring greater meaning, compassion, consciousness, and joy to your everyday life.

In Part One, we'll set the stage by seeking a deeper understanding of Leonardo's life, work, and legacy. We'll consider compelling questions about the nature of Leonardo's spirituality and his belief in God, the source of his unparalleled genius, and the mystery of his sexuality. I'll also help you decode some of the questions raised about Leonardo in the phenomenal best-seller *The Da Vinci Code* and other publications. (You needn't have read Dan Brown's novel to enjoy and benefit from this decoding.) The last chapter of Part One will introduce you to the "spiritual translation" of Leonardo's seven principles and guide you to get the most out of Part Two.

In Part Two, my intention is that you will be inspired by the Maestro to:

+ Learn practical strategies for enlivening your spiritual search.
+ Gain a deeper sense of clarity and responsibility.
+ Discover simple, compelling ways to open the doors of perception and sharpen your subtle awareness.
+ Cultivate freedom from the unconscious disowned aspects of yourself so that you can avoid sabotaging the realization of your highest ideals.
+ Enjoy the inner harmony that results from balancing the masculine and feminine aspects of your being.
+ Receive the blessings of greater energy and well-being by integrating spirit, body, and mind.
+ Deepen your experience of giving and receiving love.

DA VINCI DECODED

PART ONE

REACHING OUT
TO HEAVEN

*Occasionally heaven sends us someone who
is not only human but divine, so that through
his mind and the excellence of his intellect
we may reach out to heaven.*

—Giorgio Vasari,
Lives of the Artists

·LEONARDO·
·VINCI·

CHAPTER 1

Leonardo and the Rebirth of the Sacred Feminine

Actually, Da Vinci was in tune with the balance between male and female. He believed that a human soul could not be enlightened unless it had both male and female elements.

—DAN BROWN, *THE DA VINCI CODE*

Since the publication of *How to Think like Leonardo da Vinci* in 1998, I've traveled around the world sharing the creative inspiration of history's greatest genius with a wide range of audiences. I've addressed schoolteachers in Spokane and St. Louis, U.S. Postal Service workers in Washington, D.C., advertising executives in Slovenia, pharmacists and physicians in Philadelphia, Cancún, and Costa Rica, professors and MBA students in Charlottesville, human resource managers in Istanbul, designers and marketers

This portrait of Leonardo is probably the most accurate likeness of the Maestro, according to Professor Martin Kemp, who suggests that it may have been done by Francesco Melzi, Leonardo's closest disciple.

in London, Paris, and Portland, nurses in San Diego, company presidents in Little Rock, Las Vegas, Venice, Rome, and Madrid, gifted children in Virginia, and the listeners of countless call-in radio shows, to name just some of my audiences. The most common questions I hear from the people who call in, raise their hand, or come up to me afterward are "Did Leonardo believe in God?" and "How can you account for his genius?" (OK, some of them also ask about his sex life!) And the most frequent request I receive by e-mail from readers around the world is "Please share more on the spiritual applications of Leonardo's principles."

Then in 2003 came the publication of Dan Brown's spellbinding and phenomenally popular mystery novel *The Da Vinci Code*, and a day hasn't passed since without someone asking me, "How much of the book is true?" and "What do you think of the book?"

What I always wonder is: What would Leonardo think of it?

We do know that Leonardo da Vinci loved mysteries, riddles, and practical jokes. He loved puzzles, puns, storytelling, code making, and code breaking. This, after all, is a man who put many of his observations in mirror writing—backward writing. My hunch is that he would be delighted by Dan Brown's novel. But as for how much of it is true, well, that is another matter, and not one that Dan Brown had to concern himself with, since he was writing fiction.

Was Leonardo a member, perhaps the grand master, of the Priory of Sion, which was a secret society devoted to the protection and perpetuation of the truth of the Holy Grail? Did he possess secret knowledge of the location of the Holy Grail? Is the figure next to Jesus in Leonardo's masterpiece *The Last Supper* a woman? If so, could she be Mary Magdalene? Was Leonardo intimating that Jesus and Mary Magdalene were lovers who spawned a pure bloodline that exists to this day? Did Leonardo design a cryptex—a cipher box—like the one described in *The Da Vinci Code*? These are seductive mysteries.

Leonardo counseled that we examine anything we wish to know from at least three perspectives, so I explored these mysteries by consulting with three extraordinary resources: Professor Martin Kemp, Sir Brian Tovey, and Dr. Jean Houston.

Martin Kemp is professor of the history of art at Oxford University and author of many scholarly works on Leonardo. He was also the curator, along with Marina Wallace, of an exhibition of Leonardo's anatomical drawings at London's Hayward Gallery, and he is now organizing a multivenue global exhibition entitled "The Universal Leonardo," which is set to launch in 2006.

Sir Brian Tovey is a Renaissance art expert and visiting research fellow at the British Institute of Florence, who also happened to serve for many years as director of British intelligence. Sir Brian is a sharper, smarter, and impeccably ethical real-life version of Dan Brown's Leigh Teabing.

The third of my trio of experts is renowned anthropologist, visionary, and author Jean Houston, Ph.D. Jean, a former student of the legendary Dr. Margaret Mead, is a modern Renaissance woman and founder of a worldwide "mystery school" devoted to the exploration and understanding of the universal archetypes of wisdom as expressed in diverse cultures and traditions.

When asked about the possibility that Leonardo was a member of a secret society, such as the Priory of Sion, or that he had inserted a Mary Magdalene figure in *The Last Supper*, Professor Kemp responded, "None of the collections of Leonardo documentation (well summarized in the Metropolitan Museum's exhibition catalogue) has anything about the Priory of Sion. Leonardo had absolutely no time for such secret mumbo-jumbo.

"The figure on Christ's right is the youthful St. John, who is awaking (as traditionally) from a doze. He's typical of Leonardo's pretty young men.

"*The Da Vinci Code* is fiction not history, and I have no problem with that."

Sir Brian commented, "I have to agree with Professor Kemp that there is no evidence of Leonardo's involvement with the Priory of Sion or any similar body. I also agree with his identification of the figure on Christ's right in *The Last Supper*—an identification which has the further advantage of consistency with the account given in St. John's gospel. The myth of some kind of sexual liaison between Christ and Mary Magdalene has been around for years and lacks any kind of historical justification. And, alas, I also have to say that I have no knowledge of any activity on the part of Leonardo in the field of cryptography other than the obvious use of reverse writing in his notebooks and his intentional obfuscation of design details in many of the drawings for his remarkable inventions."

Jean Houston agreed with Professor Kemp and Sir Brian that it was unlikely that Leonardo was a member of the Priory of Sion or any other secret society. When I asked her about the possibility of a line of progeny emerging from the union of Jesus and Mary Magdalene, she suggested that it was "an enduring mystery and delicious speculation," adding that Dan Brown had placed it "where it belongs—in a novel."

Professor Kemp, Sir Brian, and Dr. Houston all agree, however, that Leonardo offers a unique inspiration to the human spirit and that there is much that we can learn from him to illuminate our consciousness and creativity.

Although many of the suppositions about Leonardo expressed in *The Da Vinci Code* are not supported by the historical record, I want to emphasize what it is that Dan Brown got so profoundly right and why I believe his story has captured the imaginations of millions. Yes, it's a well-written, action-filled page-turner with a screenplaylike feel (I can't wait for the movie!), but it's not particularly better than his other excellent mystery novels in that regard. The real power of this story is that it speaks to something deep within us. *The Da Vinci Code* taps in to what Jung called the "collective unconscious." It beckons us to become aware that we are part of a tectonic shift of consciousness. And it positions Leonardo—correctly, I believe—as the herald and prophet of the rebalancing of consciousness through the embrace of the feminine principle.

In the earliest human societies, consciousness was primarily

This is the first pure landscape by an Italian artist. Leonardo signed and dated it to record the significance of the moment. By taking Mother Earth, Nature herself, as his subject, Leonardo is expressing his attunement to the feminine principle in creation.

animistic and right-brained. Aboriginal peoples experienced themselves as one with the earth. Every tree, every animal, every cloud possessed its own sacred spirit. Mother Earth reigned. As human societies evolved, the feeling of oneness with nature was gradually replaced by the need to exercise power over it. Analytical thinking began to dominate, and paternalistic societies pushed Mother Earth into the background. This drama played out in many institutions, including, of course, the Church, as Dan Brown so vividly brings to life.

Now we are struggling toward a new synthesis; an integration of technology and soul, development and sustainability, power and altruism. Our fulfillment as individuals and our continuing survival and evolution as a species demand that we cultivate a new consciousness—one that integrates the best of the masculine and feminine ways of perceiving and being in the world.

In *The Passion of the Western Mind,* Dr. Richard Tarnas describes it this way: "The Western psyche is on the verge of an unprecedented epochal transformation: a triumphant and healing . . . reconciliation between the two great polarities, a union of opposites: a sacred marriage between the long-dominant but now alienated masculine and the long-suppressed but now ascending feminine."

The Da Vinci Code personalizes and taps in to the mystery, conflict, and drama of this "epochal transformation" as it reflects our yearning for reconciliation and partnership. The long-suppressed but now ascending, nature-affirming, goddess-worshiping feminine principle is represented, in Dan Brown's novel, by the Priory of Sion; the extreme of the long-dominant but now alienated, power-seeking patriarchy is represented by his version of Opus Dei.

If we strip away the sexual politics of our time and contemplate the eternal nature of the human psyche, we can easily see how complementary these two fundamental modes of consciousness are. The masculine mode, sometimes associated with the left hemisphere of the cerebral cortex, is more analytical, focused, and convergent; it is the mode for influencing the environment, for getting things done, for "doing." The feminine mode, sometimes associated with the right hemisphere, is more receptive, intuitive, and divergent. This is the mode for sensitivity to the environment, for letting things be, for "being." Obviously, to be whole, we must integrate the masculine and feminine principles.

There is good research-based validation for the goal of integrating masculine and feminine principles. In a landmark study at Stanford University, psychologists discovered that the highest levels of intellectual functioning are incompatible with stereotypes of masculinity and femininity. Dr. E. P. Torrance found that gender rigidity inhibits creativity. Creativity requires a balance between sensitivity, traditionally a female trait, and autonomy, a trait usually associated with males.

THE CHALICE AND THE BLADE

In her popular book *The Chalice and the Blade*, Riane Eisler traces the change in human societies from an orientation around the sacred feminine to more patriarchal modes of organization. She explores the images of the Deity as female in ancient painting, sculpture, ritual, myth, and tradition, explaining why: "It . . . makes eminent sense that the earliest depiction of divine power in human form should have been female rather than male. When our ancestors began to ask the eternal questions (Where do we come from before we are born? Where do we go after we die?), they must have noted that life emerges from the body of a woman. It would have been natural for them to imagine the universe as an all-giving Mother from whose womb all life emerges and to which, like the cycles of vegetation, it returns after death to be again reborn."

Eisler frames the "epochal transformation" that Tarnas describes as a movement away from a "dominator model" and toward a "partnership model." She defines the former as a hierarchical system, either patriarchal or matriarchal, which elevates one gender over the other. The evolving partnership model she advocates encourages "social relations [to be] primarily based on the principle of linking rather than ranking."

Like all great wisdom traditions, the Chinese philosophy of Taoism has long recognized that the balance of the masculine (yang) and feminine (yin) is a prerequisite for personal enlightenment and societal harmony. As Lao-tzu writes in the *Tao-te Ching*:

All things have their back to the female
and stand facing the male.
When male and female combine
All things achieve harmony.

Lao-tzu also emphasizes that this balance requires a rediscovery and cherishing of the sacred feminine when he writes:

The Mysterious Feminine never dies . . .
although She becomes the whole universe.
Her immaculate purity is never lost.
Although She assumes countless forms
Her true identity remains intact.
Tao is limitless, unborn eternal—
It can only be reached through the Mysterious Feminine.
She is the very face of the Absolute.

Leonardo invokes the aura of the sacred feminine in this exquisite drawing of goddesses dancing. Beyond that, the spiraling, helical, heaven-bound shapes of the women and their garments, so typical of motifs that recur throughout Leonardo's work, suggest the ultimate unity of sensuousness and sublimity.

As we struggle toward a partnership model that will require us to redefine the nature of gender roles and identities, we'll find greater harmony and increase the likelihood that we can achieve the balance between development and sustainability that is critical to getting to Level One. We are beginning to understand that integration of the masculine and feminine principles is more than just a key to individual creativity and fulfillment. It is a social and cultural imperative. And Leonardo da Vinci, as Dan Brown intuited, is humanity's supreme exemplar of this integration.

THE QUESTION OF LEONARDO'S SEXUALITY

Leonardo's sexuality may offer a clue to his extraordinary ability to express the feminine principle in his work. *The Da Vinci Code*, although a work of fiction, manages even in its contradictions to convey some of the mystery surrounding this aspect of Leonardo's life. In one place it refers to him as a "flamboyant homosexual." Yet it also depicts him as having been a grand master of the Priory of Sion, and we know from the recollections of Sophie, the female protagonist, that one of the responsibilities of the grand master was to engage in ritual heterosexual sex in front of chanting black-and-white-clad high-society cult members.

So what was the real nature of Leonardo's sexuality? We know he never married, and no one has yet claimed to have found an heir or a bloodline going back to the Maestro. Was he, as many have supposed, a homosexual? When Leonardo was twenty-four, a charge of sodomy was brought against him and a few of his friends by an anonymous accuser. But it was probably an attempt at slander aimed at one of the friends, and since it was unsupported by any evidence, all were acquitted.

It's also true that later in life Leonardo was often surrounded by beautiful young men, but the writings of those young men suggest that he was more of a father figure than anything else. As his closest disciple, Francesco Melzi (to whom Leonardo left his estate), comments: "To me he was like the best of fathers."

But maybe he was bisexual? Or perhaps he was celibate and, as Freud suggested, "transmuted his passion into inquisitiveness." Did he, as some have suggested, have a love affair with the female monarch of Mantua, Isabella d'Este? Her writings suggest that she was in love with him.

Like many of his subjects, Leonardo possessed a mysterious blend of male and female characteristics. Many contend that the *Mona Lisa* is, among its manifold meanings, a disguised Leonardo self-portrait. (See Dr. Lillian Schwartz's remarkable computer graphic comparison of the *Mona Lisa* and Leonardo's red chalk self-portrait, on page 148 of *How to Think like Leonardo da Vinci.*)

Leonardo doesn't fit neatly into our contemporary categories of gay or straight, masculine or feminine. Instead, he challenges us to seek a new way of thinking about the male and female principles and how to achieve balance between them. He puts me in mind of tantric yoga, in which masculine and feminine unite to become something divine that transcends gender.

CHAPTER 2

Leonardo's God

> We by our art may be called the
> grandchildren of God.
>
> —LEONARDO DA VINCI

Even if you're a devoutly religious person, it's hard to imagine the extent and depth of the Catholic Church's influence at the time Leonardo was born. For more than one thousand years the Church had dominated the European psyche. The threat of eternal fire in hell and the promise of redemption in heaven were overwhelmingly influential tools in ensuring obeisance to Church doctrine and power. Images of heaven and hell were everywhere, from the baptismal chapel to the burial vault. Members of every level of the Church hierarchy represented an unquestionable doctrine and were believed to possess the power to damn the disobedient to endless agony. As the great historian Will Durant noted in *The Age of Faith,* the secret of the Church's influence on the populace was its ability "to inspire absolute terror."

Although classical notions of freedom of thought, artistic expression, and humanist values were on the rise during Leonardo's lifetime, and the Florence of the Medicis was the epicenter of this rebirth, the Dominican friar Girolamo Savonarola (1452–1498) was still able to expel Lorenzo (Il Magnifico) de' Medici and his family from the city in 1494. Savonarola, who was born the same year as Leonardo, believed that he was divinely ordained to eliminate the decadent pursuit of the classical ideals of Plato and Aristotle that had been flourishing under Medici patronage. According to him, "The only good thing which we owe to Plato and Aristotle is that they brought forward many arguments which we can use against the heretics. Yet they and other philosophers are now in Hell."

In pursuit of his fanatical ideals of purity, Savonarola sent squads of children throughout the city to strip women of their fancy clothes, jewels, and makeup and to confiscate "pagan" books, paintings, and sculptures. In 1497 he organized a massive conflagration of the confiscated symbols of Florentine decadence, including paintings by the great Botticelli, Fra Bartolomeo, and Leonardo's old friend (and fellow student under Andrea del Verrocchio) Lorenzo di Credi. These brilliant artists were so cowed by their fear of Savonarola and his minions that they threw their own works onto the pyre, which became known as the "Bonfire of the Vanities."

But Savonarola made the mistake of preaching that Rome was also becoming decadent, and this did not please Pope Alexander VI. Ultimately Alexander (whose actual depravity went far beyond mere decadence) threatened to excommunicate the entire citizenry of Florence if they continued to follow

Savonarola. Although the Florentines feared damnation by Savonarola, they had an even greater terror of condemnation by the Holy See. In 1498 they made Savonarola himself the centerpiece of another public bonfire.

Even after Savonarola had been killed, his influence vanquished, and the Medicis returned to power, the dark repressiveness of fear-based religion continued to exercise a strong hold on many minds, including that of one of the greatest artists of the time and perhaps the only one whose mastery might be said to equal Leonardo's.

Twenty-three years younger than Leonardo, the stupendous genius Michelangelo was raised in the Medici household from age thirteen but grew up strongly influenced by Savonarola's fire-and-brimstone diatribes. Michelangelo was driven by an overwhelming desire to pay homage to Church teachings, as we can see in his magnificent portrayal of God bringing Adam to life in the center of the Sistine Chapel ceiling, which still serves for many as a primary visual image of the Deity. But he was also seared by guilt over his homosexuality, as we can see in his representation of himself as a flayed, hanging corpse in his terrifying *Last Judgment* on the Sistine Chapel wall. Painted nearly thirty years after his Creation scene, it conveys something of his tortured self-image and bears witness to the lingering effect of fear on his psyche.

Interestingly enough, despite his internal agonies, Michelangelo remained in the good graces of the Popes. Leonardo, however, did not always enjoy such favor. His curiosity and independent thinking, and the fact that he operated outside the fear-based paradigm of the day, often put him at odds with the Church's absolutist doctrines. Nonetheless, he did manage to avoid the fate of some of the independent thinkers who came after him, such as Giordano Bruno, who was burned alive, and Galileo Galilei, who was placed under house arrest and threatened with torture and excommunication. Leonardo was fortunate that the Inquisition wasn't yet in full swing during his lifetime. But timing alone cannot account for his immunity to persecution, which was probably owing at least in part to the care he took to avoid direct confrontation, and also to the protection he enjoyed from various powerful patrons—Lorenzo de' Medici, Giuliano de' Medici, the duke of Milan, and the king of France, among others.

But was Leonardo really a heretic? Did he believe in God? What was the nature of his spirituality?

In the first edition of his *Lives of the Artists,* Giorgio Vasari commented that "Leonardo was of so heretical a cast of mind, that he conformed to no religion whatever, accounting it perchance much better to be a philosopher than a Christian." But in a later edition Vasari tells us that before his death, Leonardo asked for the opportunity to receive the Holy Sacrament and the last rites through the Catholic Church.

We can't be sure that Vasari's later version, proclaiming Leonardo's embrace of the Catholic faith, wasn't written as a salve to Church authorities. Nor can we be sure of the absolute accuracy of either edition's account of Leonardo's life, since the first was published (in 1550) some thirty years after he had died, the second nearly twenty years after that. However, we do know that Leonardo was interred, at his request, in the cloister of the Church of St. Florentine in Amboise.

And we also know that throughout his life Leonardo questioned dogma and expressed his doubts about the literal interpretation of the Bible. For example, in the eighteen pages of the notebooks that Bill Gates purchased for $30.8 million, Leonardo questions the biblical explanation of the Flood: "Here a doubt rises, and that is: whether the Flood which came at the time of Noah was universal or not. And it would seem not, for the reasons which will now be given. . . ."

"NATURAL REASONS ARE WANTING"

"We have it in the Bible that this deluge lasted 40 days and 40 nights, of incessant and universal rain, and that this rain rose to ten cubits about the highest mountains in the world. And if it had been that the rain was universal, it would have covered our globe which is spherical in form. And this spherical surface is equally distant in every part, from the centre of its sphere; hence the sphere of the waters being under the same conditions, it is impossible that the water upon it should move, because water, in itself, does not move unless it falls; therefore how could the waters of such a deluge depart, if it is proved that it has no motion? And if it departed how could it move unless it went upwards? Here, then, natural reasons are wanting; hence to remove this doubt it is necessary to call it a miracle to aid us, or else to say that all this water was evaporated by the heat of the sun."

Not only does Leonardo question biblical literalism in terms that prefigure modern science, he also has a good time criticizing what he perceives as empty ritual, as this "Jest" drawn from his notebooks suggests:

A priest going the round of his parish on Saturday before Easter, sprinkling holy water in the houses as was his custom, came to a painter's room and there sprinkled the water upon some of his pictures. The painter, turning round somewhat annoyed, asked him why this sprinkling had been bestowed on his pictures; then the priest said that it was the custom and that it was his duty to do so, that he was doing good, and that whoever did a good deed might expect a return as good and better; for so God had promised that every good deed that was done on earth shall be rewarded a hundredfold from on high. Then the painter, having waited until the priest had walked out, stepped to the window above, and threw a large bucket of water to his back, saying: Here is the reward a hundredfold from on high as you said would come from the good you did me with your holy water with which you have damaged half my pictures.

Although Leonardo found mindless ritual a subject for mirth, there was nothing lighthearted about his treatment of religious corruption. He was outraged, for example, by the Church's practice of indulgences, which allowed people to "buy" absolution for their sins. Essentially, the Church had put a price on absolution and turned it into a thriving, high-profit-margin enterprise. As he writes: "A vast multitude will sell, publicly and unhindered, things of the very highest price, without leave from the Master of those things, which never were theirs nor within their power; and human justice will not prevent it." Leonardo referred to the "holy friars" who indulged in this practice as "pharisees." He also lamented the mass marketing of supposedly holy relics: "I see Christ once more being sold and crucified and his saints martyred."

For Leonardo spirituality was not to be found in formal rituals, relics, dogma, or a literal interpretation of the Bible. He understood the wisdom expressed by Lao-tzu:

Ritual is the husk of true faith. . . .
Therefore the masters concern themselves
with the depths and not the surface.

But in rejecting the husks, Leonardo did not throw out the divine baby with the floodwater. His spirituality resided in and was expressed through perception, awareness, and experience—the qualities that he cultivated to enrich his practice of painting. And it was when he was painting that he got beyond the surface to the depths, achieving his fullest sense of being in alignment with the wishes of the Supreme Creator, or *primo motore*. In his long *Treatise on Painting,* he described the visual arts as being the most sublime of all the arts, the one most closely "related to God":

> Do we not see that pictures representing Deity are kept constantly concealed under costly draperies and that before they are uncovered great ecclesiastical rites are performed with singing to the strains of instruments; and at the moment of the unveiling the great multitudes of peoples who have flocked there throw themselves to the ground worshipping and praying for Him whose image is represented . . . as if the Deity were present in person. It would seem, therefore, that the Deity loves such a painting and loves those who adore and revere it and prefers to be worshipped in this rather than in another form of imitation.

As the renowned Leonardo scholar Professor Martin Kemp explains Leonardo's spirituality: "He accepted that there was a supreme, ineffable power behind the design of nature, identifiable as God, but he was convinced that concrete knowledge could not reveal the nature of divinity itself. Rather, the role of human understanding was devoted to the revelations of the glories of natural design, which spoke more eloquently of divine creation than any theological book could speak of God himself."

For Leonardo, the world was alive with divine presence. Understanding that we are created in the "image of God," he devoted himself to portraying the God-like in images. In his notebooks Leonardo specifically refers to "the mind of God, which embraces the whole universe." He spent his life seeking ever-deeper union with that mind, and worshiping it through his painting.

Like St. Francis, Leonardo had an abiding love of animals and nature. And like the Hindu sage Ramana Maharshi, he expressed reverence for all life and practiced vegetarianism. (Andrea Corsalis, an Italian traveler and adventurer, wrote to Giuliano de' Medici in 1515 that, "like our Leonardo da Vinci," the Hindus revered all sentient beings, including insects.)

Like the Buddha, he counseled moderation and nonattachment to the world of materialism. He wrote, "Poor is the man who desires many things." And he added, "Neither promise yourself things nor do things if you see that when deprived of them they will cause you material suffering."

⚕ The Last Supper

Leonardo's stunning artistic genius and profound spiritual vision is evident in one of his most powerful and controversial works, *The Last Supper,* which he began in 1495 and finished sometime in 1498.

Painted on the wall of the refectory at the church of Santa Maria delle Grazie in Milan—this subject traditionally appeared in monastery dining rooms, where the monks could contemplate the sacrament as they dined—Leonardo's *Last Supper* captures, with unprecedented dramatic power, the moment in which Christ proclaims, "One of you shall betray me."

The Da Vinci Code notwithstanding, the spiritual power of this masterpiece isn't to do with the identity of the figure to Christ's right or with the mystical meaning of the letters *M* or *V,* which seem to be formed by the space between Christ and the disciples on either side. (Let's just say that *M* stands for *mystery* and *V* represents *Vinci.*) It also has nothing at all to do with the absence of a chalice (numerous precedents exist in Italian paintings of the Last Supper, known collectively as *cenacoli*) or the presence of a disembodied dagger-wielding hand. (Early copies of the original and preliminary drawings by the Maestro demonstrate unequivocally that the hand and dagger are St. Peter's. This was Leonardo's homage to the gospel passage in which Peter draws his sword to defend his Savior.)

Perhaps one way of understanding *The Last Supper*'s effect on us is to observe the contrast between Christ's sublime and transcendent tranquillity and the turbulent sea of human emotion and agitation surrounding him. Leonardo captured in words the everyday humanity he succeeded so brilliantly in conveying in paint when he described his plans for the painting. Referring to the figures of the apostles to either side of Christ, he wrote in his notebook:

> One of them, who was drinking, has left his glass in its place and turned his head toward the speaker. Another links his fingers tightly and turns with a frown to his companion; another holds out his open palms, shrugs his shoulders up to his ears, and gapes with astonishment. Another whispers to his neighbor as the taller turns toward him to lend an ear, holding a knife in one hand and in the other a half-cut loaf. Another, while turning round, knife in hand, upsets with his hand a glass over the table. Another lays his hands on the table and stares, another chokes over his mouthful of food, another leans forward to see the speaker.

Another way of understanding what Leonardo achieved is through an examination of the iconography of the painting, which plays upon one of Leonardo's favorite images—the rippling circles of water that emanate from the center when a stone is dropped into a still pond. As he noted:

> Just as the stone thrown into the water becomes the center and cause of various circles, and the sound made in the air spreads out in circles, so every body placed within the luminous air spreads itself out in circles and fills the surrounding parts with an infinite . . . number of images of itself, and appears all in all in each part.

If you look carefully at the table at which Christ and the disciples are seated, you'll see that everything on it is circular—rolls, glasses, plates—and all these circles echo and repeat each other as they progress from the central figure of Christ. The disciples also seem to flow out in a wavelike pattern from Jesus. In *The Last Supper* Leonardo has made Christ the still "center and cause" from which all infinity flows. And he brings us the moment in which Christ spoke his prophetic words to his disciples, a divine stone tossed into the pool of time, prefiguring the Resurrection and rippling through eternity to grace human destiny forever.

CHAPTER 3

The Source of Genius

> *He who has access to the fountain*
> *doesn't go to the waterpot.*
>
> —LEONARDO DA VINCI

Leonardo da Vinci is generally recognized as the greatest all-around genius in human history. He operated on all channels, at the very highest level, and always sought to express the deepest inner realities of all his subjects. In addition to his genius for art, science, and invention, Leonardo was also renowned for his musical talent, his personal charm, and his extraordinary strength, physical beauty, and grace. Vasari tells us that "he made every sorrowful soul serene" and that he "sang divinely without any preparation at all." Vasari also extols Leonardo's "great personal strength [which] was joined to dexterity" and his "great physical beauty . . . and more than infinite grace in every action." Kenneth Keele, anatomist and curator of one of the most comprehensive exhibitions of Leonardo's anatomical works, calls him "a unique genetic mutation." And Johann Wolfgang von Goethe sums it up by referring to Leonardo as a "model of human perfection."

The young Leonardo wrote in his notebook, "I wish to work miracles," and in many cases he appears to have succeeded.

LEONARDO'S MIRACLES

+ In his "Codex on the Flight of Birds," he recorded minutiae about the movements of feathers and wings in flight that could not be confirmed or fully appreciated until the development of slow-motion moving pictures over four centuries later.
+ Many of his anatomical drawings are uncannily accurate and rival modern X rays. He was the first to accurately portray the child in the womb, the first to make casts of the brain and the ventricles of the heart, and a pioneer of comparative anatomy. He also noted that arteriosclerosis causes premature death and could be prevented by moderate exercise and improved diet.
+ He designed and may have built a telescope. (His notebook jottings read: "make glasses to see the moon enlarged.")
+ His aerial perspective maps of Imola and other cities are works of incredible scope and perception.

- His art changed the way we see the world. His *Mona Lisa* is humanity's most familiar and most imitated work of art, and his *Last Supper* may be the greatest painting ever created.
- Forty years before Copernicus he noted (in capital letters, for emphasis) "Il SOLE NO SI MUOVE" (The sun does not move).
- He was the first to describe the phenomenon of soil erosion and the first to describe the system of leaf arrangement in plants.
- He was the first to declare, in terms that are still used today in the physics classroom, that the angle of incidence is always equal to the angle of reflection.
- He designed a photometer to measure the intensity of light, which prefigured by three hundred years the one invented by Benjamin Rumford.
- He created designs for the parachute, extendable ladder, ball bearing, diving bell, snorkel, gearshift, olive oil press, scissors, adjustable monkey wrench, automated loom, hydraulic jack, canal lock, and many more amazing inventions.

How can we explain Leonardo's range and depth of talent, his incomparable gifts in so many diverse areas? What's the source of his unprecedented—and as yet unequaled—multifaceted genius?

Many people have tried, with varying degrees of success, to understand Leonardo. Sigmund Freud's book *Leonardo da Vinci and a Memory of His Childhood* offers a fascinating but ultimately unsatisfying analysis of the Maestro's psyche and oeuvre, focusing not so much on his genius but on his deficiencies. In his attempt to "explain Leonardo's inhibitions in his sexual life and his artistic activity," the founder of psychoanalysis attributes the Maestro's tendency to leave works unfinished to his ambivalent feelings about his illegitimacy and his parents' separation.

Freud based much of his book on his interpretation of a dream Leonardo recorded in which a bird—a vulture, according to the German translation that Freud used—flew down from the sky and struck him repeatedly on the inside of his lips with its tail. To reach his conclusions about Leonardo's psyche, Freud makes much of the Egyptian mythology involving vultures. Unfortunately, the translation of Leonardo's notebooks that Freud used was incorrect. In recounting his dream Leonardo used the word *nibbio,* which is a kite—another type of bird of prey—not a vulture.

Freud's failings can be traced to more than just the faulty translation of Leonardo's notebooks upon which he relied, for even with better data his reductionist approach couldn't do justice to Leonardo. (One might also suspect that Freud may have been just a bit envious of Leonardo's supreme talents.)

The details of Leonardo's childhood are sketchy, but we do know that his mother, Caterina, was a peasant from the village of Anchiano and his father, Ser Piero, who was not married to Caterina, was an upper-middle-class but otherwise unremarkable accountant and notary from Vinci. Ser Piero sired a total of twelve children, but none of Leonardo's siblings was especially gifted. Leonardo received nominal education in mathematics, reading, and writing (in Italian) and never attended university. Although he prided himself on being a *uomo senza lettere* (man without academic training) and a *disciepolo della sperienza* (disciple of experience), Leonardo did teach himself Latin later in life so that he could read the classics.

But despite this unimpressive background, Leonardo was clearly blessed from a very young age with abilities that were extraordinary—in one case in particular, so astonishing as to be frightening, as Giorgio Vasari relates:

> It is said that when Ser Piero da Vinci was at his country villa, he was sought out at home by one of his peasants, who had with his own hand made a small round shield from the wood . . . and who wanted Ser Piero to have it painted . . . he was delighted to do this, since the peasant was very experienced in catching birds and fish and Ser Piero made great use of him in these activities.

Vasari explains that Ser Piero brought the shield to his young son Leonardo and asked him to paint something on it. Leonardo straightened the crooked wood over a fire and then smoothed it out and prepared the surface with gesso. Vasari continues:

> He began to think about what he could paint on it that would terrify anyone who encountered it and produce the same effect as the head of the Medusa. Thus, for this purpose, Leonardo carried into a room of his own . . . crawling reptiles, green lizards, crickets, snakes, butterflies, locusts, bats, and other strange species . . . and by adapting various parts of this multitude, he created a most horrible frightening monster with poisonous breath that set the air on fire. And he depicted the monster emerging from a dark and broken rock, spewing forth poison from its open mouth, fire from its eyes, and smoke from its nostrils so strangely that it seemed a monstrous and dreadful thing indeed.

Upon completion of the work, Leonardo invited his father for a viewing.

> He arranged the shield on his easel . . . and shaded the window to dim the light, and then he had Ser Piero come inside to see it. At first glance, Ser Piero . . . was immediately shaken, not realizing that this was the shield, nor that what he saw drawn was a painting. And as he turned and stepped back, Leonardo stopped him and said: "This work has served the

purpose for which it was made. Take it away, then, and carry it home with you, for this was the intended effect."

Vasari relates that besides having the artistic talent to make a painting so lifelike that it frightened its viewers, the young Leonardo also confounded his schoolmasters with the profundity of his questions about mathematics and other subjects.

QUESTIONABLE ATTRIBUTIONS

Leonardo's actual achievements are without parallel. But, because of his seemingly superhuman abilities and what Professor Kemp refers to as the "compelling power of absent evidence," he is sometimes credited with achievements for which there is very little actual basis. Most prominent among these are the following:

+ The creation of the Shroud of Turin (an intriguing idea, but highly speculative)
+ The design of the Stradivarius violin (Leonardo did design and build a number of wonderful instruments, but this probably wasn't one of them)
+ The invention of the bicycle (the drawing in his notebooks is a forgery)
+ The design of the helicopter (Leonardo's helical screw hints at the principle that allows a helicopter to fly, but unlike his parachute or glider, it doesn't accurately prefigure the real invention)

Leonardo demonstrated a level of genius inexplicable in ordinary terms. Thus Dr. Deepak Chopra refers to Leonardo as "an accelerated expression of the natural evolution of consciousness." And Jean Houston comments, "This is the mind of a Maker in its most consummate form. This is a man who is co-creating with God." She adds, "People gifted with this Renaissance capacity are tapped in to parallel dimensions and can co-create with the Vast Intelligence."

The realm of Vast Intelligence is what Jung referred to as the *mundus imaginalis*. Physicist David Bohm termed it "the implicate order." Deepak Chopra describes it as "pure potentiality." And Leonardo's ability to "tap in to" the Vast Intelligence is what made his extraordinary body of work possible, by giving him access to a realm of artistic truth few others have glimpsed.

"Everything he touched turned to eternal beauty," legendary art critic Bernard Berenson offered as a poetic review of Leonardo's accomplishments. Implicit in his words is a fundamental truth about the Maestro: his gifts and his works were manifestations of an unusually pure connection to the Divine.

Leonardo's gifts emerged from this Source. The purpose of this book is to guide you to use his inspiration and example to allow you to become more receptive to that same Source.

The Divine Source of Creativity

"Every house is built by some one, but the builder
of all things is God."
—*Christianity, Hebrews 3:4*

"This universe hath sprung from the Lord. In him it is
established. He is the Cause of Creation."
—*Hinduism, Vishnu Purana*

"All things originate from heaven."
—*Confucianism, Li Chi*

"It is he who made the earth by his power,
who established the world by his wisdom,
and by understanding stretched out
to the heavens."
—*Judaism, Jeremiah 10:12*

"Praise be to God, who created the heavens and the
earth, and ordained the darkness and the light!
He it is who created you."
—*Islam, Koran, sura 6*

CHAPTER 4

*H*ow to Find the Grail

> *Men go to see mountains and valleys,*
> *but pass themselves by.*
>
> —ST. AUGUSTINE

In Dan Brown's *The Da Vinci Code* the protagonists, Harvard symbologist Robert Langdon and French cryptologist Sophie Neveu, find themselves caught up in a whirlwind of intrigue and danger as they seek to track down the Holy Grail and prevent it from falling into the wrong hands. While evading Paris's top police detective and a fanatical, murderous albino sent by Opus Dei, they follow clues written in blood and invisible ink provided by Sophie's murdered grandfather, who served dual roles as curator at the Louvre and grand master of the Priory of Sion. After decoding an anagram that guides them to clues hidden behind the *Mona Lisa*, they are eventually led to a vault in a private bank, where they find the special cipher box—supposedly designed by none other than Leonardo da Vinci—that holds the secret of the Grail. But as Joseph Campbell writes in *The Power of Myth*, "The Grail . . . is that which is attained and realized by people who have lived their own lives. The Grail represents the fulfillment of the highest spiritual potentialities of the human consciousness."

It Is Within You

"What the undeveloped man seeks is outside, what the advanced man seeks is within himself."
—*Confucius*, Analects

"The kingdom of God cometh not with observation: neither shall they say, lo here! Or, lo there! For, behold, the kingdom of God is within you."
—*Christianity*, Luke 17:20–21

"He is seated in the hearts of all."
—*Hinduism*, Bhagavad Gita

"On God's own nature has been molded man's."
—*Islam*, Hadith

"God created man in His own image, in the image of God created He him."
—*Judaism*, Genesis 1:27

"His light is in every heart."
—*Sikhism*, Guru Nanak

Leonardo may actually have designed a cryptex, or cipher box, like the one described in *The Da Vinci Code,* although there is no concrete evidence to support this idea. But in any case, as Leonardo knew very well, to find the secrets of the Grail you must look outside the box and inside yourself. This is the meaning of Paulo Coelho's enchanting fable *The Alchemist,* in which a young shepherd sets out on a perilous pilgrimage through Egypt to seek a magnificent treasure, only to discover that it was hidden in his own backyard. Coelho's fable echoes the classic Buddhist story of a young prince who sets out on a journey to find a precious jewel beyond any price, only to realize that it was sewn into the lining of his coat from the beginning.

In other words, the treasure, the jewel, the Grail, are all within. This is universal wisdom, echoed in every tradition.

In the following pages, we'll explore how you can use Leonardo's inspiration and example to "reach out to heaven," to awaken and nurture your spiritual growth. We'll seek to open ourselves to the same Source that Leonardo drew upon to liberate his remarkable gifts. And we'll be guided in the search for the Grail within each of us by Leonardo's seven principles.

The seven principles that I first described in *How to Think like Leonardo da Vinci* emerged from an intensive study of the Maestro's life and work. In addition to studying his words, I consulted with and read the writings of many distinguished scholars. I attempted to walk in his footsteps and see the world through his eyes. I went to his birthplace in Anchiano and to the place he died in Amboise, and I contemplated his original works in galleries around the world. I started dreaming about him, and from those dreams, and careful thought based on the research, the seven principles emerged with great clarity.

Seven is a powerful, special number. In addition to being the limit (plus or minus two) of short-term memory, as defined in a famous study done at Harvard, it is also the number of:

Days of the week
Notes in the Western musical scale
Innings to wait before stretching in baseball
Days for God (including His day of rest) to create the
 world
Pillars of wisdom in Proverbs
Branches of the Tree of Life in the Kabbalah
Years the Buddha sought enlightenment
Times the Buddha circled the bodhi tree
Steps in spiritual evolution according to Sufism
Chakras, or wheels of energy, from the Hindu tradition
Sacraments in Catholicism
Trumpets sounding on Judgment Day
Stars Christ held in his hand in the Book of Revelation

In the quest to understand Leonardo's approach, after discovering seven principles I tried to find an eighth principle, and also attempted to consolidate down to six. But it couldn't be done. There are seven principles, irreducible and complete. I describe them below, summarizing how Leonardo embodied each one in his life and offering their "translation" into spiritual terms.

1. **Seek the truth (*curiosità*).** An insatiably curious approach to life and an unrelenting quest for continuous learning. *Curiosità* is the wellspring of lifelong learning and creativity, so it is fitting that Leonardo may have been the most curious person who ever lived. *Curiosità* is also the expression of our yearning for connection with the Divine.

2. **Take responsibility (*dimostrazione*).** A commitment to test knowledge through experience, persistence, and a willingness to learn from mistakes. By rejecting dogma and superstition, Leonardo took responsibility for his own search. The spiritual journey requires us to

take responsibility for our thoughts and actions, and ultimately for all of creation.

3. **Sharpen awareness** (*sensazione*). The continual refinement of the senses, especially sight, as the means to enliven experience. Leonardo noted that "the five senses are the ministers of the soul." He penetrated into the depths of creation by honing his awareness.

4. **Engage the shadow** (*sfumato*). A willingness to embrace ambiguity, paradox, and uncertainty. Leonardo's search for light led him beyond the embrace of ambiguity, paradox, and uncertainty. His quest led him, literally and figuratively, to engage and understand darkness. This is often the missing link in the spiritual path.

5. **Cultivate balance** (*arte/scienza*). The balancing of left- and right-brain thinking, culminating in whole-brain thinking. Leonardo's persona and work express more than just a balance between logic and imagination, science and art; they represent the essential balance of the masculine and feminine principles in creation.

6. **Nurture integration** (*corporalità*). The integration of mind and body through the cultivation of grace, ambidexterity, fitness, and poise. Leonardo's outstanding physical gifts and remarkable insights into anatomy, healing, and wellness were an expression of his integration of body, energy, and spirit.

7. **Practice love** (*connessione*). A recognition and appreciation of the interconnectedness of all things and phenomena; systems thinking. Leonardo knew that "everything connects to everything else." He was pointing toward an understanding that all of creation is linked and that the universe is an expression of divine love.

In Part Two, we'll explore the seven principles as they apply to your spiritual development. Each principle will be introduced with a single image created by Leonardo and elaborated through powerful words drawn from the world's great wisdom traditions. We'll consider how each principle manifested in Leonardo's work and how it links to timeless, universal spiritual understanding. Then you'll have the opportunity to contemplate a simple self-assessment designed to help you deepen your understanding of the presence of the principle in your life now, followed by some practices to help you become more susceptible to grace. Each chapter will conclude with another Leonardo image to inspire you while doing the practices.

A FEW POINTERS
FOR GETTING THE
MOST FROM PART TWO

You can approach the following chapters in Part Two in any order you like, but I do recommend that you read them all before beginning the spiritual practices. After you have read all seven chapters, return to the one that beckons you most and reread it. Then contemplate the self-assessment and explore the practices that you feel are most inviting. The self-assessments are not tests, but rather statements for you to reflect upon. You'll get the most from them if you take some time to contemplate each one, rather than just accepting your first reaction. The practices are not intended to offer a comprehensive program for your spiritual unfolding. Rather, they're designed to give you a taste of the spiritual implications of each of Leonardo's principles and to whet your appetite for further exploration. Each chapter offers a connection to practical resources (listed at the back of the text), which can guide you to more in-depth applications.

PART TWO

THE SPIRITUAL SECRETS OF LEONARDO'S SEVEN PRINCIPLES

The caterpillar which through the care exercised in weaving round itself a new habitation with admirable design and fine workmanship, comes out of it afterwards with painted and beautiful wings, rising on these toward heaven.

—Leonardo da Vinci
on transformation

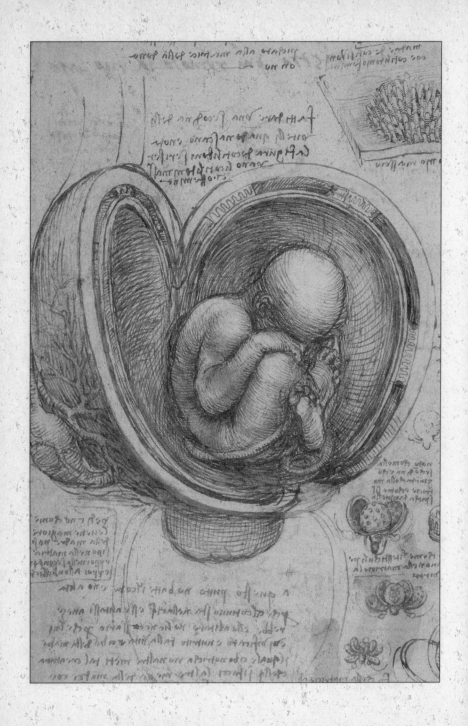

CHAPTER 5

S eek the Truth (Curiosità)

If . . . thou seek the Lord thy God,
thou shalt find him, if thou seek him with
all thy heart and with all thy soul.

—DEUTERONOMY 4:29

Leonardo sought, with unrelenting passion, to understand the origin of life and the secrets of creation. His drawing of the human embryo is the first accurate representation of the subject and an unforgettable symbol of his incomparable *curiosità*, his lifelong search for truth. Though we tend to take knowledge of the anatomy of the child in the womb for granted now, imagine the sense of discovery and excitement Leonardo must have felt when he first saw the details of this miracle.

For Leonardo, the Divine was

As Professor Martin Kemp writes, "No drawing of an embryo in a womb ever came closer to capturing the very spirit of generation."

manifest in nature and was to be worshiped through close study and reverent appreciation of nature's perfection. In his notes accompanying this amazing drawing, Leonardo writes: "Though human ingenuity may make various inventions answering by different machines to the same end, it will never devise an invention more beautiful, more simple, more direct than does nature; because in her inventions nothing is lacking, and nothing is superfluous."

He then offers specifics about the development of the embryo, referring to the *primo motore*—interestingly enough!—with the feminine pronoun: "She needs no counterpoise when she creates limbs fitted for movement . . . but puts within them the soul of the body which forms them, that is the soul of the mother which first constructs within the womb the shape of man, and in due time awakens the soul that is to be its inhabitant. And this at first lay dormant, under the tutelage of the soul of the mother who gives it nourishment and life through the umbilical vein with all its spiritual members."

Leonardo's drawing of the embryo reminds us that we all come from the same Source. It beckons us to revitalize our birthright of *curiosità*. All of us are born with dynamic curiosity, the desire to explore, know, and understand, to seek the truth—though few of us keep it as alive within as Leonardo did. In the words of Glen Doman, of the Institute for the Achievement of Human Potential: "Every child is born with the potential genius of Leonardo da Vinci, and then we go about de-geniusing them."

Doman adds, "Learning is the greatest game in life and the most fun. All children are born believing this and will continue to believe this until we convince them that learning is very hard work and unpleasant. Some kids never really learn this lesson and go through life believing that learning is fun and the only game worth playing. We have a name for such people. We call them geniuses."

Doman is renowned for his pioneering work helping brain-damaged children to recover normal functioning. In his classic book *How to Teach Your Baby to Read* Doman tells the story of a child named Tommy who was sent to him with a bleak prognosis: he would never function normally or be able to read. After Tommy's parents worked with him, applying Doman's approach for a few years, Tommy was not only functioning but was actually reading two years above grade level at school. If a brain-damaged child can learn to read two years beyond his grade, then what are so-called normal children capable of accomplishing? Doman's work offers hope for more than just brain-damaged children; it provides inspiration for all of us.

For twenty-five years I've been traveling the world attempting to inspire people to awaken their potential. Not surprisingly, many people start out somewhat skeptical. Most of us wouldn't claim to be geniuses. But ask parents about the first moment they looked into their new baby's eyes: almost everyone acknowledges seeing the spark of genius there. And many will go further and say that they saw something divine.

You were born with that divine spark, but not with the secrets of how to overcome the "de-geniusing" effects of schooling and society. That has to be learned. The Sufi poet Jalaluddin Rumi describes how to free the God-given gift of genius when its source is blocked:

> For the other kind of intelligence is the gift of God:
> its fountain is deep within the soul.
> When the water of God-given knowledge
> surges from the breast,
> it never stagnates or becomes impure.
>
> And if its way to the
> outside is blocked, what harm is there?
> For it flows continually from the house of the heart.
> The acquired intelligence is like conduits
> Which run into the house from the streets:
> if those pipes become blocked, the house
> is bereft of water.
> Seek the fountain within yourself.

Rumi's exhortation to "seek the fountain within yourself" invites us to energize our spiritual *curiosità,* to reawaken the childlike qualities of openness, innocence, and inquiry that come from the "house of the heart."

Similarly, the Bible urges us to "become as little children" in order to enter the kingdom of heaven. And Zen Buddhism guides us to release our preconceptions and embrace "beginner's mind." A childlike curiosity, sense of wonder, and passion for learning are the wellsprings of spiritual growth. As Sigmund Freud noted, "The great Leonardo continued to play as a child throughout his adult life, thus baffling his contemporaries."

Please think back to your childhood, and try to remember at what age you began wondering:

+ Where did I come from?
+ Why are we here?
+ What happens when we die?
+ Is there a God?
+ Does my life have a meaning and purpose?
+ Does the soul exist?
+ Who am I?

Many people stop asking these questions, or look to others for the answers, as they become distracted by the demands of making their way in the world. Inevitably, however, events occur in our lives—a loved one dies, we become seriously ill, a job is lost, or a marriage falls apart—and we begin to contemplate the great questions again.

Please don't wait for a traumatic event to put you on the path to seeking meaning. This kind of questioning drives you toward awakening and is the beginning of the rediscovery of your spiritual *curiosità.*

Becoming a seeker, embracing the search for truth, wanting to know, is the *primo motore* of the spiritual journey. The primary importance of seeking the truth is reflected in all the world's sacred traditions.

WISDOM IS FOUND BY
THOSE WHO SEEK HER

✦ The Christian gospel of Matthew urges: "Seek ye first the kingdom of God, and His righteousness; and all these things shall be added unto you," and "Seek and ye shall find. Knock and it shall be opened unto you."

✦ The Buddhist scripture, the *Dhammapada*, proclaims, "He who applies himself to the doctrine of truth, illuminates this world like the moon set free from the clouds."

✦ Islamic Hadith counsel us to "seek knowledge from the cradle to the grave." And they comfort us with this divine invitation: "He who approaches near to Me one span, I will approach to him one cubit, and he who approaches near to me one cubit, I will approach near to him one fathom; and whoever approaches Me walking, I will come to him running."

✦ And from the Jewish tradition, Solomon teaches: "Wisdom is radiant and unfolding and she is easily discerned by those who love her, and is found by those who seek her. She hastens to make herself known to those who desire her. . . . To fix one's thoughts on her is perfect understanding. . . . The beginning of wisdom is the most sincere desire for instruction."

> "I reveal to men the origin of their cause of existence."
> —*Leonardo da Vinci*

Leonardo's quest for truth took him up into the heavens and deep beneath the oceans. He roamed the countryside asking questions about things he did not understand: How were mountains and valleys formed? Why was a bird able to sustain itself in the air? What is lightning, and how does it relate to thunder? Throughout his life Leonardo probed the secrets of nature with unrelenting *curiosità*.

His curiosity about nature went hand in hand with his most important question: What is the nature of the human soul? This core question drove him to plumb the secrets of the womb and of birth, to explore the anatomy of the moment of death, and ultimately to capture in his paintings a depth of soul that had never before been expressed.

> "A good painter has two chief objects to paint,
> man and the intention of his soul;
> the former is easy, the latter hard."
> —*Leonardo da Vinci*

What if you could search for the truth of your own soul, for the experience of the Divine within, with some of the same spirit of *curiosità* that the Maestro brought to his investigations?

Seek the Truth: Self-Assessment

∞

☐ I keep a journal or notebook to record my observations, insights, and questions concerning my spiritual growth.

☐ I listen to the questions little children ask and aim to incorporate the same openness, innocence, and curiosity in my spiritual quest.

☐ I take adequate time on a daily basis for contemplation and reflection about the nature of my soul's true calling.

☐ I cultivate practical ways to be more receptive to the subtle promptings of my soul.

☐ I seek to free myself from unconscious, habitual patterns of thought and behavior that impede my awareness.

☐ I seek a deeper awareness of the spiritual dimension of my experience every day.

☐ I am willing to look objectively at all the different aspects of myself, including those that I don't like.

"Good men by nature wish to know."

—LEONARDO DA VINCI

KEEP A SPIRITUAL NOTEBOOK

Although geniuses throughout history have almost always kept notebooks, Leonardo's more than six thousand pages of notes are, as Professor Martin Kemp emphasizes, without parallel. (And Kemp and other scholars estimate that up to 80 percent of his notes may have been lost!)

Leonardo's notebooks express the freedom and intensity of his *curiosità* across a phenomenal range of subjects, from the essence of light and the flow of water to the visual expression of the human soul and the nature of birth and death. He referred to the essentially spiritual benefits of keeping a notebook in this poetic pun: "Feathers shall raise men even as they do birds, toward heaven, that is by letters written with their quills."

When I realized at age nineteen that my path through life was to be focused around questions of personal growth and spiritual exploration, I started to keep a notebook. On the first page I wrote this quote from Hermann Hesse's *Demian:* "All I ever wanted was to live from the promptings of my true self, why was that so very difficult?" For many years it did seem quite difficult. The good news is that living from my true self has become easier. And the practices offered in this chapter will, I hope, make it easier for you, too.

Your practical exploration of the spiritual application of Leonardo's principles will be enhanced by working with your own notebook. Rather than focusing primarily on the external world, however, this "spiritual notebook" will be used to record elements of your inner journey. As Herman Hesse writes in *Demian:* "I have been and still am a seeker, but I have ceased to question stars and books; I have begun to listen to the teachings my blood whispers to me."

Please take some time to consider the questions below and record your reflections in your notebook. Let's start with the most basic question: Who are you?

To begin to answer that question is to understand how infinite the expressions of self can be. Your body has changed and will continue to change. From day to day you experience moods, emotions, and inner states that sometimes differ so radically that you may even seem to be different people in different circumstances. Changing jobs or careers, getting married or divorced, losing or gaining weight, moving from one house or apartment to another—all these external changes can alter you inwardly, just as inner change can alter you externally. But is there something inside you that always remains the same? If so, what is it? How would you describe it? How do you know who you are?

+ Do you identify your self through your thoughts?
+ Do you identify your self through your feelings?
+ Do you identify your self through your body?
+ Do you identify your self with something other than your thoughts, feelings, and physical being?

Another way to approach these fundamental questions is to use the analogy of music. If you think of your psyche as an orchestra, you might view its various parts as being comparable to the string section, woodwinds, brass, chorus—and we all have a percussion section.

+ Who is the conductor?
+ What refrains does the chorus return to over and over again?
+ Who is the composer?

Looking for the answers to these questions will take time. Seekers must cultivate the ability to listen and look within. A simple way to begin is through the practice of self-observation.

WE HAVE MULTITUDES WITHIN US

Our greatest self-delusion is the belief that we are one integrated consciousness, that when we say "I" we are always talking about the same personality. As Dr. Robert Ornstein of the University of California Medical Center and author of *The Evolution of Consciousness* emphasizes, "Our natural view of our mental state is deeply distorted . . . the oneness we feel is an illusion . . . we are not the same person from day to day or moment to moment. Our mind contains a special system, hidden from our view, that quietly preserves the illusion of unity."

SELF-OBSERVATION PRACTICE

Leonardo was the first Italian painter to make a landscape the sole focus of a work of art. He observed the natural world with a remarkably penetrating and objective curiosity. Spiritual growth requires us to take the same kind of curious, nonjudgmental attitude toward our inner landscape. But all of us are susceptible to filtering our self-perceptions through our ego-based, subjective preconceptions.

Have you ever, for example, observed yourself in a videotaped coaching session, perhaps intended to help you improve your presentation skills or your golf game? Most people are surprised to discover that what they appear to be doing on the video screen differs considerably from what they imagined themselves to be doing. This type of discrepancy manifests in our inner lives as well.

You can close the gap and begin to see yourself more clearly by practicing self-observation. Self-observation is a powerful tool for focusing your spiritual *curiosità*. Choose a theme for the day or the week and record observations in the spirit of that theme in your notebook. You can jot down your thoughts throughout the day or just make mental notes to be recorded in your notebook at a quiet time before sleep. Aim to make simple, accurate observations. Avoid speculation, opinion, and theory, and focus on noting your observations with what Leonardo called *ostinate rigore* (obstinate rigor). You'll get the most from this practice if you approach it as though you were observing someone else rather than yourself.

When I first began this kind of work thirty-two years ago, the theme my teacher assigned for self-observation was nonjudgmental awareness. We were asked to observe ourselves and notice the ways in which we filtered our experience through the lens of judgment. I was surprised and humbled to discover that almost everything I perceived was automatically assigned to a category of like/dislike or good/bad.

You may wish to experiment with this theme for self-observation. You can begin by considering:

+ How your judgment of liking versus disliking and good versus bad affects your experience
+ How your experience of living might change if you suspended the filters of like/dislike and good/bad

Self-observation is a core discipline of spiritual *curiosità*. Learning to look at yourself objectively liberates tremendous energy for inner unfolding and transformation. When working with the theme of nonjudgmental awareness, please be alert to the tendency to judge how well you are applying the practice. If you discover yourself thinking something like "I'm lousy at non-judgmental awareness" or "I rock at this!" it's a good opportunity to laugh at yourself and refocus on objective self-observation.

Do this exercise on your own or with a friend and compare notes.

BYRON KATIE'S FOUR-QUESTIONS PRACTICE

Byron Katie is an enlightened teacher whose work represents the heart of spiritual *curiosità*. Katie's potentially life-transforming approach is based on four simple questions that guide you toward inner freedom, and they are relevant to genuine seekers from all traditions.

The four questions will, as Katie expresses it, "burn up anything that isn't true for you. They'll burn through to the reality that has always been waiting."

The four questions are:

1. Is it true?
2. Can you absolutely know that it's true?
3. How do you react when you think that thought?
4. Who would you be without the thought?

Katie's fifth step is to "turn around" the proposition under investigation.

We'll use the four questions to explore an issue from your life to help you get a taste of how it works. Let's start with something that almost everyone experiences from time to time: the feeling of anger, hurt, or rejection that comes from the perception that we are not being appreciated by someone close to us.

Please think of an example from your own life and express it as a proposition, such as "Because _____ doesn't appreciate me, I feel resentful toward her/him."

After you've written your proposition (it's a good idea to say it aloud as well), you can begin to "burn through it" by asking the first of the four questions.

1. *Is it true?* Ask yourself, "Is it true that _____ doesn't appreciate me?"

Ask the question in the pure spirit of *curiosità* and then listen within until an answer arises. As Katie comments, "If you really want to know the truth, the answer will rise to meet the question."

The second question enhances the depth and focus of the inquiry.

2. *Can you absolutely know that it's true?* Read your proposition again, and consider whether you can really know if it's true that "_____ doesn't appreciate me."

Is it actually possible for you to be certain that someone does or does not appreciate you? Do you ever have feelings of admiration and respect for someone and discover later that that person had no idea how you felt?

The third question helps you discover the effect that your proposition has on you.

3. *How do you react when you think that thought?* In other words, when you think of your proposition, what do you experience, and how does it affect the way you interact with the person in question?

Katie suggests that you make a list of your reactions. Examples might include such responses as: "I give _____ the silent treatment," "I withhold my own expressions of appreciation," or "I try harder to be pleasing to gain more appreciation." Continue this exploration as fully as you can, including consideration of how you act toward yourself in circumstances when you feel unappreciated. Examples might include: "I get depressed," "I feel bad about myself," or "My stomach starts to hurt." Go deep inside yourself. Seek to listen to your innermost thoughts to understand how you react when you believe your proposition.

The fourth question takes you to the core of your being.

4. *Who would you be without that thought?* What role
   does the proposition play in your self-identification?
   Who would you be if you let go of the notion that
   "_____ doesn't appreciate me"?

With eyes closed, conjure up the scene of that person not ap-
preciating you. Imagine, as you visualize the scene, that the
thought of being unappreciated doesn't exist. Go further and
imagine that the thought that you *should* be appreciated doesn't
exist. Take all the time you need to embrace the disappearance
of your proposition. Pay attention to the nuances of your response to question four. What happens to your feelings and your
internal experience of spaciousness?

The fifth step asks you to "turn it around." In other words,
take your original proposition, "_____ doesn't appreciate me,
which makes me feel resentful toward him/her," and experiment with reversing it: "I don't appreciate _____, which
makes him/her resent me."

Could that be true? Could your own lack of appreciation, or
failure to express appreciation, have affected the other person's attitude toward you? In other words, could the two of you be locked
in a mutually self-defeating circle of behaviors? Look for other examples of ways in which your own lack of appreciation for that
person (and others) might be creating an unwelcome dynamic.

Another powerful turnaround might be something like: "I resent myself because I don't appreciate myself." Is it possible that
could be true, or perhaps truer than your original proposition?

After contemplating a few turnarounds, the inquiry continues
along similar lines. As Katie expresses it: "Turnarounds are your
prescription for health, peace, and happiness. Can you give yourself the medicine that you have been prescribing for others?"

Katie and her collaborator Stephen Mitchell, the renowned
translator of the *Bhagavad Gita* and *Tao-te Ching,* have produced a
marvelous guide to this enlightening process of spiritual *curiosità,*
entitled *Loving What Is: Four Questions That Can Change Your Life.*

❧ Innocence

Leonardo's magnificent drawings and paintings of children express more than just his exceptional talent for accurate representation of external features. He also expressed the inner beauty
and soul of innocence. One step toward entering the kingdom of
heaven is to become like a little child, to experience a renaissance
of your innocence through spiritual *curiosità*.

Begin by spending time with youngsters and seeking to learn
from them. On the day I started writing this book, I happened to
be staying with friends who have a beautiful five-year-old daughter
named Julia. As we were finishing dinner, Julia went around the
table and gave everyone a kiss good night. I asked her, "What time
will you be up in the morning?" "I sleep late," she replied. Her
mom explained that "late" meant 6 a.m.! So I said, "Good, I'll get
to see you again in the morning." And Julia answered, "Yes, I'll be
resting in bed listening to my heart." My conversation with Julia
reminded me to take some time every day to do the same.

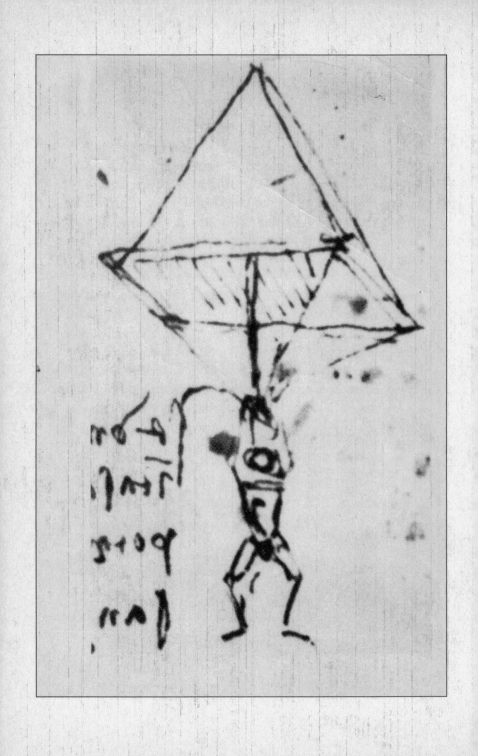

CHAPTER 6

Take Responsibility (Dimostrazione)

> *What proceeds from you will return to you.*
>
> —MENCIUS, CONFUCIAN SAGE

In one of humankind's most innovative leaps of invention, Leonardo da Vinci designed a parachute before anyone could fly. Modern engineers have confirmed that the proportions he indicated actually work. As the Maestro noted next to his drawing of the parachute, "If a man have a tent of linen without any apertures, twelve ells [27 ft] across and twelve in depth, he can throw himself down from any great height without injury."

Leonardo's fragile, enchanting drawing represents more than just a fantastic leap of imagination and innovation. It also symbolizes, in poignant fashion, the existential courage needed to take

The Maestro was fascinated by the dream of flight, spending years on the study of aerodynamics. He made many sketches for flying machines, and, in a marvelous leap of imagination, he drew this remarkable parachute.

responsibility for the spiritual quest. Leonardo's parachute suggests the notion that we are suspended in what may seem like a vast emptiness, hanging by thin cords of hope as we depend on grace—and the 144 square ells of cloth that Leonardo's scientific observations led him to specify—to keep us afloat. Although contemplation of the immensity of the cosmos can cause us to feel alone and insignificant, we must nevertheless accept the challenge of opening our minds and hearts to the mysteries of the universe.

Leonardo was willing to take responsibility for constructing a fresh, original view of the world, relying on the wisdom generated by his observations and his experience. Emerging from the darkness of the Middle Ages in Europe, when the idea of individuality as we understand it didn't exist, when all authority was vested outside of the self, when it was rare for anyone to question anything, Leonardo dared seek his own answers. He questioned the excesses and power politics of the religious establishment of his day while also rejecting superstition, alchemy, and astrology (although the ledgers found in his notebooks do reveal that on a few occasions he may have indulged in consultations with "fortune-tellers"). He noted that "many have made a trade of delusions and false miracles." And he warned against "the contradictions of the sophistical sciences which lead to eternal quackery."

Leonardo had the courage to seek always to look at things as they are. His willingness to reject imitation, question authority, and think for himself would be remarkable in any age; it becomes even more amazing when one considers that he was heir to a thousand-year tradition of believing that everything worth knowing was already known.

Before, during, and after Leonardo's time, Church authorities enforced the idea that if observed experience contradicted dogma, the dogma must prevail. For Leonardo, however, it was the principle of *dimostrazione* that prevailed. His unparalleled independence of mind, persistence, and reliance on firsthand observation and experience combined to create in him a profound sense of responsibility. He knew that despite all external pressures to conform to dogmatic views, he was ultimately responsible for generating his own ideas and forming his own judgments.

Leonardo embodies the wisdom of the Sufi proverb "He who tastes, knows." We also find echoes of his emphasis on experiential knowing in the words of our own Walt Whitman:

> You shall no longer take things at second or
> third hand, nor look through the eyes of
> the dead, nor feed on the specters in books,
> You shall not look through my eyes either,
> nor take things from me,
> You shall listen to all sides and filter them from yourself.

Leonardo urged his students to become *inventore*—original thinkers who would, as he did, question the accepted theory and dogma of the time and "filter" for themselves. He wrote, "No one should imitate the manner of another, for he would then deserve to be called a grandson of nature, not her son. Given the abundance of natural forms, it is important to go straight to nature." And that was exactly what he did when he undertook his pioneering scientific deconstruction of the biblical story of the Flood. Having considered the evidence, Leonardo comments that such belief in the literal truth of the Flood "can not exist in brains with any extensive powers of reasoning."

> "O human stupidity! Do you not perceive that you have spent your whole life with yourself, and yet you are not aware of the thing you chiefly posses, that is of your folly."
> —*Leonardo da Vinci*

Leonardo's spirit of independence didn't come without a cost. He was so far ahead of his time in so many areas that he may have been one of the loneliest people who ever lived. Biographer Dmitri Merejkowski described him as someone who awakens too early while everyone around him is still sleeping.

But Leonardo never lost the courage to continue to search for truth despite much adversity. Although he noted that great sensitivity can be the cause of great suffering, the overall tone of his writings suggests an indomitable spirit. In 1499, after investing sixteen years of devoted labor to create a full-size clay model for a magnificent twenty-four-foot-tall bronze sculpture of a horse in Milan, he saw his work destroyed by invading French troops, who used it for target practice. Leonardo wrote: "About the horse I shall say nothing as I know the times." The invasion also cost him the support of his patron Ludovico Sforza, the duke of Milan, who fled the invaders, leaving his court behind. Leonardo effectively became a refugee after Ludovico's departure, moving from city to city all over Italy for a number of years. He faced many other challenges during the course of his sixty-seven years, including being imprisoned in Florence as a young man before allegations against him of being a homosexual were dismissed; losing his patron at the Vatican, Giuliano de' Medici (brother of Pope Leo X), through premature death; the ruination of his masterpiece painting *The Battle of Anghiari* because of a problem with the technique he used to dry the paint; the scheme by his half brothers to cheat him out of his share of his father's estate; the stroke that paralyzed the right side of his body three years before his death as an exile in France; and, of course, the failure of his dream of flight.

In the face of these and many other challenges, Leonardo writes notes of encouragement, affirmation, and inspiration to himself: "I shall continue," "I never tire of being useful," "Obstacles do not bend me," "Every obstacle is destroyed through rigor," and "Fix your course to a star and you can navigate through the storm." The star to which Leonardo fixed his course was his intellectual rigor, his freedom from preconceived ideas or opinions.

THE DREAM OF FLIGHT

Some chroniclers believe that one of the Maestro's disciples may have attempted to test his flying machine, with disastrous results, by launching it from the top of Monte Ceceri, a hill outside Florence. Although Leonardo's dream of flight didn't come true in his lifetime, one of his wing designs was recently reconstructed by a British air-sports company and tested in Sussex by world hang-gliding champion Judy Leden. It worked! Leden commented, "My first reaction was that I was stunned by the beauty of the thing. It was a bit scary when they said I shouldn't fly any higher than I was prepared to fall, as the glider would probably break up with my weight, but it proved to be much stronger than modern hang gliders."

Leonardo's design for the parachute was also recently tested by another Briton, sky diver Adrian Nicholas. Nicholas strapped on a 187-pound wood and canvas pyramidal parachute built according to the Maestro's directions and using materials available in cinquecento Milan. He then jumped out of a hot-air balloon from a height of ten thousand feet in South Africa's Mpumalanga Province, descending gently for eight thousand feet before deploying a modern parachute to land. Nicholas described the experience as "incredibly moving . . . I had a feeling of gentle elation and celebration. It was like floating under a balloon. I was able to stare out at the river below, with the wind rattling through my ears. As I landed, I thanked Leonardo for a wonderful ride."

Leonardo knew that enlightenment was predicated on keeping an open mind. "The greatest deception men suffer is from their own opinions," he wrote. As Seng-Ts'an, the Third Patriarch of Zen Buddhism, expresses it, the beginning of enlightenment is to "merely cease to cherish opinion."

Beyond that, however, Leonardo knew that God helps those who help themselves and that this could sometimes be hard work.

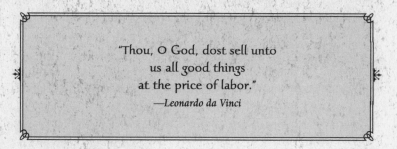

"Thou, O God, dost sell unto
us all good things
at the price of labor."
—*Leonardo da Vinci*

The labor that brings us all good things is more than just our effort in the outer world—it is also a reflection of our inner work and ethical awareness. Leonardo emphasized that "justice requires power, insight and will." He admonished his students to recognize that "he who does not punish evil commends it to be done." And he counseled, "He who walks straight rarely falls."

In his delightful book entitled *Essential Spirituality*, Roger Walsh explains the importance of taking responsibility for our intentions and actions toward others. "This general psychological and spiritual principle—what we intend for others we create for ourselves—is one of the most powerful and important yet, sadly, also one of the least understood and appreciated of all spiritual principles. Once it is understood, it transforms the basis of all relationships. The great secret of ethics is, as the Buddha pointed out: 'Whatever you do, you do to yourself.' "

Another way of expressing this is through the Hindu tradition's law of karma, which serves as a universal feedback system on the effects of our thoughts, feelings, intentions, and actions. The law of karma—what goes around comes around—offers us a compelling spiritual imperative for self-examination. Only when we explore the relationship between our intentions and their effects, in the full light of consciousness, will we achieve the realization of our highest dreams. As Leonardo noted, "You can have neither greater nor lesser dominion than you have over your self."

WE REAP WHAT WE SOW

+ As the psalm from the Hebrew tradition expresses it: "Thou renderest to every man according to his work."
+ The Christian gospel of Matthew proclaims: "He shall reward every man according to his own work."
+ The Confucian sage Mencius phrases it thus: "What proceeds from you will return to you."
+ And from the Hindu *Garuda Parana*: "Everyone reaps the fruit of their own deeds."

Leonardo chose to ask big questions—about the origin of life, the secrets of flight, the nature of the soul, the essence of beauty, and the meaning of death. Throughout his life he navigated deep currents of uncertainty, basing his ideas on his day-to-day observations even as his spirit soared beyond the stars. Leonardo's example is the undying embodiment of Jean Houston's exhortation to let our minds be "stargates."

Leonardo beckons you to wake up, think for yourself, and take responsibility for opening *your* stargate to experience the world in all its freshness and beauty.

Take Responsibility: Self-Assessment

- ☐ I have formulated my own understanding of spirituality based on my own experience.

- ☐ I distinguish between superstition, religious belief or observance, and spiritual experience.

- ☐ I strive to test my spiritual understanding through my actual experience.

- ☐ I take responsibility for my thoughts.

- ☐ I take responsibility for my emotions.

- ☐ I take responsibility for my body.

- ☐ I take responsibility for my intentions.

- ☐ I take responsibility for the results I achieve in my life.

- ☐ I accept the religious teachings with which I was raised.

- ☐ I reject the religious teaching with which I was raised.

- ☐ I seek a reconciliation between the religious teaching with which I was raised and my actual experience.

❧ Take Responsibility: Spiritual Practices

> *"Man is worthy of praise and blame solely in*
> *respect of such actions as it is within*
> *his power to do or abstain from."*
>
> —LEONARDO DA VINCI

THE FRANKL CONTINUUM

In one of the *Star Trek: Voyager* episodes featuring the holographic Leonardo, Captain Janeway exclaims that the Maestro was one of her childhood heroes. He was mine, too, along with another great hero of spiritual *dimostrazione*, Viktor Frankl, whom I discovered when I was fourteen and struggling to escape the sense of meaninglessness that had overcome me when I learned about the Holocaust. Frankl, author of *Man's Search for Meaning*, was an Austrian psychiatrist who was imprisoned in a Nazi concentration camp during World War II. While living under the most horrific conditions imaginable, Frankl realized that although his captors had taken his liberty, they could not deprive him of his inner freedom. He created a system of psychotherapy called logotherapy, based on organizing one's life around this inner freedom. Frankl wrote, "Everything can be taken from a man, but one thing: the last of the human freedoms—to choose one's attitude in any given set of circumstances."

Frankl is a rare example of someone who, under terrible circumstances, actually applied Gandhi's wisdom that "we must be the change we wish to see in the world." Like Leonardo and Gandhi, Frankl offers a profound inspiration for taking responsibility by exercising our inner freedom. Whenever I face adversity and am tempted to complain or blame someone else for my situation, I think of Frankl and immediately shift my attitude.

Of course, most of us are blessed with a level of external freedom and relative comfort that can obscure the importance of our spiritual *dimostrazione*. Moreover, our litigious, entitlement-oriented culture can seduce us into thinking that others owe us something, that we should look outside ourselves for what we need. Our sense of personal responsibility is diminished by such thinking.

What I call the Frankl continuum is a way of measuring the extent to which we can consider ourselves conscious, responsible beings. You can think of it as a line moving from left to right in increments from 0 to 100 percent. The far right, the 100 percent mark, is the realm of those who, like Frankl, Leonardo, and Gandhi, take full responsibility for their thoughts, intentions, actions, and effects on others.

The far left, 0 percent, is the realm of whiners and blamers who think and act as though everything is someone else's fault. This is the consciousness of the thief who breaks into your house, trips on the furniture while attempting to rob you, and then sues you for damages. (Actually, that's 1 percent; zero is the lawyer who represents the thief.)

How can you recognize where you are on the continuum? You can assess your responsibility by monitoring your attitudes as they are reflected in your language, and then rating yourself on the continuum from 0 to 100 percent. Classic lines spoken by those at the lower end of the continuum include:

"My wife / husband doesn't understand me."
"I can't get anyone at work to listen."
"If only . . ."
"I can't . . ."
"There's nothing I can do about it."
"They won't let me."
"He makes me furious."

If you catch yourself saying any of the above or indulging in any other form of whining, blaming, complaining, or commiserating (being miserable together), do not at first attempt to change. Instead of grafting superficial positive thinking on top of your current real feelings, just observe or witness the whining. The difference is that now you are conscious, so you are free to choose to whine. Of course, once you are aware, whining starts to get a little boring. So once you have acknowledged, accepted, and chuckled about the part of you that loves to whine, you become able to choose a more constructive orientation.

Some reflections from the higher end of the continuum include:

"I am choosing my response to this person or situation."
"I teach people how to treat me."
"I can only change others by changing the way I see them."
"How can I alter my approach to generate better results?"
"How does what I detest about this person or situation mirror something in my own character?"

Now choose a challenging experience from the past year, perhaps a difficulty at work or a problem in an important personal relationship, and describe your reaction to it in your notebook. Consider your reaction objectively, as though you were observing someone else, and note where you are on the Frankl continuum. Then rewrite the story of that experience, imagining that you chose things to happen exactly as they did. For example, you might describe a situation in which a relationship ended and notice that you initially framed it as though "he/she left me," portraying yourself as a passive recipient of another's choice. But look again and consider the idea that you chose to be with someone who would ultimately leave. Could it be possible that some part of you actually wanted the person to leave? Are there any benefits that have emerged from the person's leaving? By choosing to be responsible for the results in your life, you develop your ability to make wiser choices.

THREE-PERSPECTIVES PRACTICE

Leonardo's magnificent drawings of a flower symbolize his method of learning from experience. He looked at everything—flowers, faces, the parts of the body that he portrayed in his anatomical studies—from at least three perspectives so that he could free himself from preconceptions and prejudices and see things more clearly. In his *Treatise on Painting*, for example, he explains that because "mistakes are more easily detected in the works of others than in one's own," one must first look at one's work from a physical distance, then observe its reflection in the mirror, and then, after taking some relaxation to further open and clear the mind, one must seek the opinions of another and listen with receptivity.

> "Therefore by my [anatomical] drawings every part will be known to you, and by all means of demonstrations from three different points of view of each part."
>
> —*Leonardo da Vinci*

Leonardo's discipline of threefold perspective is as important in the mastery of the inner world as it is in the accurate representation of the external world. The Dalai Lama, a contemporary paragon of spiritual *dimostrazione*, explains why in this excerpt from his book *The Art of Happiness*:

The ability to look at events from different perspectives can be very helpful. . . .One must realize that every phenomena, every event, has different aspects. For example, in my own case, I lost my country. From that viewpoint, it is very tragic—and there are even worse things. There's a lot of destruction happening in our country. That's a very negative thing. But if I look at the same event from another angle, I realize that as a refugee, I have another perspective. As a refugee there is no need for formalities, ceremony, protocol. . . .When you are passing through desperate situations, there's no time to pretend. So from that angle, this tragic experience has been very useful to me. Also, being a refugee creates a lot of new opportunities for meeting with many people. People from different religious traditions, from different walks of life, those who I may not have met had I remained in my country. So in that sense it's been very, very useful.

Of course, when we are under stress or facing pain, disappointment, or loss, it can be very difficult to think like Leonardo or the Dalai Lama. Our attention narrows, and it's easy to feel victimized by events that we cannot control. But we can control our response to events, especially if we train ourselves in the discipline of enlarging our perspective when we are under more normal conditions.

You can begin to integrate this attitude of inner freedom and responsibility so that you can draw on it under stressful circumstances by experimenting with the attitude that all of your experiences are opportunities for you to grow and learn. Just as the Dalai Lama described the challenging situation of being exiled from his country, please:

+ Choose a challenging situation from your current life and describe it briefly in your notebook.
+ Explore your assumptions and feelings about the challenging situation.

The Dalai Lama acknowledged the difficulties and tragedies associated with the foreign domination of his homeland, and then he looked at the effect of these events from the perspective of growth and learning and expressed his awareness of the benefits that accrued—meeting others, rejecting pretense, being freed from formal structures. Please attempt to do the same with the challenging situation from your life.

+ Look at the situation from three different perspectives. What are three other assumptions you could make about this situation?
+ What new information emerges from these three perspectives, and how does that impact your thoughts and feelings about it? Please record your reflections in your notebook.

My friend Jill (not her real name) graciously agreed to share her notebook entry expressing her application of the three-perspectives exercise as it applied to the situation of her divorce from her husband of twenty years. During the year before they separated, she had become aware that he was emotionally involved with another woman, but when she confronted him about it, he denied it, and she declined to take a stand out of fear that he would choose the other woman over her. Soon she learned that he had introduced this other woman to one of his children and discussed with her the fact that he was unhappy in his marriage. Although he didn't tell Jill that he wanted a divorce, he did say that he did not intend to celebrate their upcoming twentieth anniversary and began to talk of a trial separation. Then, after more than twenty years of resisting couples therapy, he finally agreed to go. In therapy he denied that he was there to end the marriage, said he was open to whatever outcome might happen, and told Jill that he loved her. But as she put it, "He danced around answers to very direct questions, never making a clear declaration of desire or intent." She felt that the real reason he had agreed to therapy was so that the therapist would help him out of the marriage. In the end it was Jill who made the decision to divorce, thus allowing him to deny any personal responsibility for the breakup. Her ex-husband is currently in a relationship with the other woman, and Jill has had a very hard time dealing with both the loss of someone she loved and the lack of clarity, if not downright dishonesty, about the situation that led to that ending. Her notebook records the way her use of the three-perspectives exercise enabled her to move from a feeling of victimization to empowerment and forgiveness.

PERSPECTIVE 1: BLAME

He is a man who claims that he values his integrity immensely—he claims that is all someone has in life; yet I experience him as having little to none. I do not perceive myself to be a saint by any means, but we had relationship agreements in place that I believe he violated. I thought him to be manipulative, cagey, and passive-aggressive in dealing with our relationship as he orchestrated a decision for divorce. He put a lot of artful gloss on the basic reality: he cheated on me, and I blame him for it. And for a while I blamed myself—obviously he would not have been enticed away if I had been a better wife, met his needs, kept quiet about my own, etc. I also blame myself for letting him get away with it for so long. The problem is that the feeling of righteousness I get from blaming him isn't very fulfilling or constructive; blaming leaves me feeling angry and unhappy with both of us.

PERSPECTIVE 2: PERSONAL ACCOUNTABILITY
When I look at the situation through the lens of personal accountability, it appears quite different. When I met him he was still married. I met his children and was living with him at the time he was filing for divorce. Except for the excuse of youth, how could I not have known that this could likely repeat itself?

I wasn't happy for most of our marriage. The degree of intense, rugged individualism that characterized my husband's behavior only increased my huge longing for intimacy and connection. I allowed us to live parallel lives, often acquiescing to his desires and making the unacceptable acceptable to such a point that I didn't even realize the degree to which I damped down my own needs. I found some growing, healthy ways and some unhealthy, dysfunctional ways to cope with the pain and anxiety—no matter what I did, I never found the courage to draw a clear line in the sand, to take a stand for our relationship in a way that could have resulted in calling it quits even earlier. I say this without blaming myself or him—just as a matter of noticing what was. Perhaps it was I who facilitated his orchestration of separation and divorce because I didn't have the courage to make that move.

In any case, I see that I chose him and that the issues that led to the demise of our partnership were evident from the beginning. I chose to collude with his antics over the years. And I recognize my consistent choice to disempower myself through fear—the fear of rejection that I might experience if I challenged him even though I was experiencing the rejection in a more insidious way all along. The good news is that by embracing my sense of choice around all this, I feel that I have reclaimed my power. I experience intense feelings of anger from time to time, but I'm also experiencing the least amount of anxiety that I have felt in twenty-five years.

PERSPECTIVE 3: BLESSING

When I first looked at this situation from the perspective of being responsible for my choices, it was hard—like taking medicine. It felt so easy to just blame and suffer. But as I've reinforced the notion of my own responsibility for all this, I've found it easier to forgive him and myself and to consider the blessings that have accrued from this drama. Perhaps he came into my life as a teacher, a facilitator, a friend, a passionate partner, a person to grow up with (I was only twenty-four when we met), to gain a wonderful family from (three amazing stepchildren with whom I'm still very close). Perhaps I intuited that we had a road to travel until we came to the end of the road and that the adventure down the road had enormous intrinsic value, no matter how difficult it was at times. Although we had quite an amicable divorce, there has been immense pain and investment in recovering—all fodder for learning. And I do not mean that in a glossed-over Pollyanna kind of way, nor am I bitter. Truly, had it not been for his immense independent streak—which ranged from everything from being away much of the time to finances to self-disclosure to not including me in his life or with his friends—I would not have taken accountability for fulfilling my own wants. And even if he allowed greater dependency upon him (at least financial), it would not have substantially changed the quality of intimate connection—we would have likely wound up in the same situation. Yet I began to take care of my own needs to a greater degree. While still married, I bought a home, because I wanted roots versus what we could do in the house we were leasing. I created my own community of friends and a satisfying career. Yes, there is still pain; however, that is part of life. As the Buddhist saying goes, "Pain is inevitable; suffering is optional." I feel so much more empowered when I consider that things transpired just as they did for good reason and when I recognize that we each had full accountability in this situation. I choose to embrace the path of personal growth and consciousness—making the most of all these experiences to be truer to myself, to listen and follow the promptings of my soul every day so that I can fully savor all my blessings.

Multiplying Your Angles of Vision

"If you look from a different angle . . .
you will find that the act which has made you angry
has also given you certain opportunities, something
which otherwise would not have been possible. . . .So
with effort you'll be able to see many different angles
to a single event. This will help."

—*Dalai Lama*

THREE-CHAIRS PRACTICE

This is another version of the three-perspectives practice, especially useful for gaining insight into the mind of someone with whom you are in conflict. Think of a person with whom you are having some kind of difficulty. It could be your boss, your spouse, your parent, your child, your friend—anyone whose actions or attitudes are troubling to you.

1. Describe the problem in your notebook.
2. Set up three chairs, two facing each other and one off to the side in a witness position. (Or, if you like, you can just do this in your imagination.)

3. Sit in the first seat. Imagine the other person sitting in the seat facing you. Say nothing, but keep gazing quietly at the person. What are your feelings as you sit there? What would you like to happen? Record any insights in your notebook.

4. Move to the seat across from yours and imagine you are the other person. Pretend that you can see yourself in front of you as the other person would. Put yourself completely in the other person's shoes (this is easier if you adopt a body posture that you associate with the other person). What are the other person's thoughts, feelings, dreams, and desires concerning the situation? What does the other person most want? What are the facts as the other person sees them? What feelings and opinions do you experience as the other person? In your notebook write about the situation from the other person's perspective. When you are finished, take a moment and sit quietly, and consider if this alternative perspective has led to any surprises or new insights.

5. Move to the third seat (the observer). Adopt the persona of someone not involved in the situation. It could be anyone, real or imaginary. You can adopt any persona you like in this position—a wise person, a friend, a figure from history. (Perhaps Leonardo da Vinci?) Now imagine seeing yourself and the person with whom you are struggling sitting facing each other in the two chairs in front of you. Describe what you see. What does each of them really want? What are they missing about the situation? As a wise observer, what do you want for both of them? What have they forgotten? Are they missing anything about the situation that might be helpful to them? Record your thoughts from the observer's perspective.

What have your learned from switching chairs? What is different about the situation? What is the same? How do you feel about it now? Do you have any new ideas about approaches or a different course of action? What is your responsibility and best course of action now? Record your thoughts in your notebook, or just let them percolate in your psyche for a while, until they become part of you.

> **6.** If you like, you can take one more perspective. Imagine a divine, angelic presence floating above all the chairs. This observer looks at the situation from the perspective of highest good for all in the situation. Ask yourself what the angel would say.

FIX YOUR COURSE TO A STAR: CINEMA VERITÉ

Hasidic wisdom informs us: "No limits are set to the ascent of man, and the loftiest precincts are open to all. In this, your choice alone is supreme." Leonardo's life became an ascent to the loftiest precincts because he chose to make the ascent. We are drawn to him because he reminds us of our own potential to reach for the stars.

This is a simple practice for shifting your perspective and clearing out interference with your power to choose a life that reflects your highest aspirations. It is also fun, especially if you like movies.

Please begin by musing on these questions:

+ What if all your memories were nothing more than wisps of illusion in your imagination?
+ Somewhere inside could there be a more "real" part of you, one that is more than the sum total of the superficial roles you play or the events that happen to you?
+ Does your life sometimes feel like a movie—with someone else as the director?

After allowing the questions to resonate within you, please try the following exercise. Sit comfortably and enjoy a few full, easy breaths. Close your eyes, and as you relax, imagine viewing your life as a movie. Allow key experiences from your childhood and school days to appear on your imaginary screen. Watch as your major life milestones, tragedies, accomplishments, mistakes, and memories of relationships, family, friends, joy, and sorrow all pass before you. Avoid analyzing or getting too caught up in any particular scene.

When the movie reaches the moment you are in now, press your mental pause button and bring your attention back to your breathing. Now, if you had to categorize the movie you just saw, how would you describe it? Is it a tearjerker, comedy, film noir, action-adventure movie, romance, art film, or horror flick? If the movie had a director, would it be Scorsese, Allen, Wilder, Peckinpah, Spielberg, Fellini? Now imagine redoing your life movie in a different genre and with a different director. View your imaginary life film from this alternative perspective.

Next, please imagine that this moment, right now, exists independent of the scripts you just saw acted out. Go further and imagine that your existence has only just begun in this moment. In the freshness of this virgin moment, what do you choose for your life now? What do you choose for the remaining scenes of your personal movie? Please write your responses in your notebook.

> "If you understand spiritual practice in its
> true sense, then you can use all twenty-four hours of
> your day to practice. True spirituality is a mental
> attitude that you can practice at any time."
> —*Dalai Lama*

CHAPTER 7

Sharpen Awareness (Sensazione)

> *The eye with which I see God is the same eye that*
> *sees me. My eye and the eye of God are one eye,*
> *one vision, one knowledge, one love.*
>
> —MEISTER ECKHARDT, CHRISTIAN MYSTIC

The angel on the left, part of *The Baptism of Christ* by Verrocchio, is the first authenticated painting by Leonardo da Vinci. Leonardo painted the angel while he was an apprentice in Verrocchio's workshop. In the Renaissance, it was not unusual for a master to ask an aspiring adept to finish off some details of a painting. But in this case the results were unusual indeed, because Leonardo's work so clearly surpasses that of his teacher.

When I first saw this painting on a visit to Florence's Uffizi Gallery (designed, incidentally, by Vasari), I experienced

Close up of angels from
The Baptism of Christ by
Verrocchio

something extraordinary and unforgettable: I felt as if I were in the presence of an angel. With its rapturously attentive gaze directed toward the sacrament and its face filled with a look of reverent enthusiasm, Leonardo's angel expresses the essence of spiritual *sensazione*. By contrast, Verrocchio's angel is dull and distracted—like "a bored choirboy," as critic Robert Wallace has commented.

Leonardo's angel stands out not only for its brilliance in contrast to the other figures painted by Verrocchio, but for a beauty I consider to have eclipsed every other work I saw in the entire treasure house of the Uffizi.

Apparently Verrocchio himself had a similar reaction. Giorgio Vasari relates that when the "True Eye" saw the delicate, exquisite, and numinous quality of his pupil's work, he retired from painting.

Leonardo also painted a portion of the landscape behind his angel. Legendary art critic Lord Kenneth Clark describes it as "full of movement, light moving over hills, wind stirring the leaves of trees, water flowing and falling in cascades; all of which is rendered in brilliant broken touches, with scurries and flutters of the pen, or flicks of golden paint from the brush." Clark adds that the work demonstrates "the prophetic power sometimes found in the earliest work of genius."

Leonardo's first painting is of course an eloquent testimonial to his precocious artistic talents, but it also vividly expresses his spiritual sensitivity, for it emerged from a plane of perception and awareness that was beyond his teacher's imagination. As Jean Houston comments, "The other-worldly beauty of the landscape, and the lucidity of light emanating from Leonardo's angel, accurately reflect the inner light of the enlightened soul."

We are all endowed, like Leonardo and the angel he created, with the capacity for engaging the world around us through a lively, radiant, even rapturous attention. Or we can fall into the bored and dull mode of mindless habit, barely registering our surroundings. The choice is ours.

If we make the choice to sharpen our awareness, we expand our ability to see things afresh, as children do—and as geniuses do. Poet William Wordsworth, recounting what he recalled of the "dream-like vividness and splendor which invest objects of sight in childhood," brought these early days back to life with his vivid description of the radiance that lit them from within:

> There was a time when meadow, grove, and stream
> The earth and every common sight,
> To me did seem
> Apparelled in celestial light,
> The glory and the freshness of a dream.

Alas, such radiance of vision is usually lost once childhood is past. As Leonardo lamented five hundred years ago in Tuscany, the average person "looks without seeing, listens without hearing, touches without feeling, eats without tasting, moves without physical awareness, inhales without awareness of odour or fragrance, and talks without thinking." Let his assessment serve as a compelling invitation to sharpen your awareness and cultivate mindfulness in your everyday life. To do so is to celebrate the presence of the Divine in all that you see.

> "There is a light that shines brighter than the sun,
> brighter than the light in the highest heavens.
> It is the light that shines within your heart."
> —*Upanishads*

We can, of course, begin to sharpen awareness by cultivating the refinement of all our senses, as Leonardo did. He enhanced his already extraordinary sensory acuity with Olympian zeal. This allowed him to see things that no one else could see, such as the details of a bird's subtle movements in flight, the nuances of the ebb and flow of water in a stream, and the true nature of the diffusion of light in a sunset.

The Maestro nurtured his perceptual sensitivity by creating an environment that was aesthetically uplifting: he worked to the sounds of fine music, took delight in graceful movement, enjoyed the feel of the finest fabrics he could afford. He created his own cologne made from lavender and rosewater, savored the aroma and taste of simple but fine food, and surrounded himself with elegance and beauty in every way possible.

He did all this not just for the intrinsic joy of such pleasures but because he believed that "the five senses are the ministers of the soul."

> "What mind can penetrate your nature? What language can express this marvel [the miracle of sight]. None, to be sure. This is where human discourse turns toward the contemplation of the divine."
> —Leonardo da Vinci

To spiritualize *sensazione*, we must refine our awareness to ever more subtle levels, including but not limited to the realm of the five senses, as we awaken the inner eye and survey the landscape of the soul. The Sufi Barqi points the way with the provocative notion that "aesthetics is only the lowest form of the perception of the real." Plato calls us to discover the "eye of the soul," referring to it as "more precious than ten thousand bodily eyes, for by it alone is truth seen." And Lao-tzu says simply, "A sensible person prefers the inner to the outer eye."

Saper vedere (knowing how to see) was one of Leonardo's mottoes. And knowing how to see encompasses the cultivation of the eye of the soul, the inner eye. But how is the inner eye to be developed? Although there is no packaged program, here are a few clues that we'll look at in more depth in the practices section of this chapter.

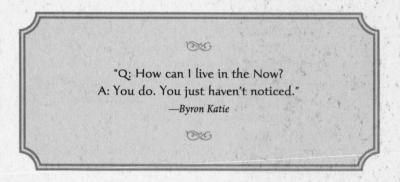

"Q: How can I live in the Now?
A: You do. You just haven't noticed."
—*Byron Katie*

The first clue is to be fully mindful in the present moment. This moment, now, is the only moment, always. Leonardo noted that "in rivers, the water that you touch is the last of what has passed and the first of that which comes; so with time present." Every tick of your watch takes place now. And so does every breath. (The word *spirit* comes from the Latin word *spirare*, "to breathe.") Mindfulness is complete attention in the now, rather than worrying about the past or investing in expectations about the future.

Another clue is to cultivate an attitude of reverent appreciation of all of creation. As we look beyond the surface to sense the soul of every living creature, we encounter our own soul. Leonardo describes this form of awareness thus: "The lover is moved by the thing loved, as the sense is by that which it perceives and it unites with it and they become one and the same thing."

Many traditions counsel asceticism as a means to develop deeper awareness and spiritual insight. Gandhi exemplified this path and lived by the motto "Renounce and rejoice." Fasting, simplicity, and silence can be great teachers, but when they become ends in themselves they can lead to a spiritual cul-de-sac.

Rabindranath Tagore, the Nobel prize–winning poet who gave Gandhi the name "Mahatma" (great soul), sees the pleasures of the senses as divine gifts that are to be cherished because of their source. He rhapsodizes:

> Deliverance is not for me in renunciation. I feel the embrace of freedom in a thousand bonds of delight. Thou ever pourest for me the fresh draught of thy wine of various colors and fragrance, filling this earthen vessel to the brim. My world will light its hundred different lamps with thy flame and place them before the altar of thy temple. No, I will never shut the doors of my senses. The delights of sight and hearing and touch will bear thy delight. Yes, all my illusions will burn into illumination of joy, and all my desires ripen into fruits of love.

The Buddha lived the sixth-century equivalent of a playboy lifestyle before renouncing earthly pleasures and entering a period of intensive self-denial and asceticism. But once his enlightenment came, he taught the path of the Middle Way. The core of the Middle Way consists of being fully conscious in any given moment. Whether you choose to fast, to eat a simple meal, or to indulge in a lavish meal isn't as important as the commitment to experience your choice in a spirit of gratitude and joy.

In every moment we have the opportunity to contract or expand our awareness. Invite the spirit of Leonardo's angel into your life now, expanding into the reverent consciousness that draws you closer to the light within.

Sharpen Awareness: Self-Assessment

❧

☐ What percentage of my time is devoted to thinking or worrying about the future?

☐ What percentage of my time is devoted to thinking or worrying about the past?

☐ What percentage of my time is devoted to the present moment?

☐ My senses are becoming sharper and my awareness is expanding as I get older.

☐ I seek practical ways to sharpen my awareness.

☐ I am aware of the effects of my everyday environment on my consciousness.

☐ I seek to see the world around me in a fresh, open way every day.

☐ I seek to see the world inside me in a fresh, open way every day.

☐ I am aware of the flow of my breath and the beating of my heart.

✣ Sharpen Awareness: Spiritual Practices

*"For him who has perception a mere sign will suffice. For him
who does not really heed, a thousand explanations are not enough."*

—HAJJI BEKTASH, SUFI TEACHER

CULTIVATE *MEMORIA*

In his classic work *The Brain Book,* Peter Russell points out that
research into the nature of memory shows that we are more
likely to remember things that come first and last in a series. The
tendency to remember what comes first is called the "primacy
effect," and the tendency to remember what comes last is called
the "recency effect."

Memoria is the Italian word for "memory" or "remembrance."
It is a word that appears many times in Leonardo's notebooks. We
can enrich our inner lives and sharpen our awareness by taking advantage of the way *memoria* works, focusing on key points of primacy and recency throughout the day to remind us to be more
open to grace. This is what many religions do by teaching us to
pray at beginnings and endings, openings and closures, both small
and large, daily and cyclical, seasonal and annual. These moments
are enshrined in rituals that give their followers repeated reminders
of the presence of the Divine as they go about their daily lives.

You can sharpen your spiritual awareness by consciously af-
firming your connection to the Divine at key points of primacy
and recency throughout your day.

The Jewish tradition, for example, teaches that "the key to
everything is the way you start." At the door of every Jewish home
you'll find a mezuzah, a small box with a scroll of blessing inside.
The mezuzah serves as a reminder of the Divine each time one enters or leaves. For Sufis, Tibetan Buddhists, and many others, all ac-
tivities begin and end with a prayer of dedication. Dining, working

on a project, exercising, meditation, and yoga practice all begin and end with a dedication. Before dining, for example, you might give thanks and then dedicate the nourishment you will receive to a higher purpose, such as "May this food be transformed in me for service to my Creator." You can repeat a similar dedication as you finish your meal. At the beginning of meditation or yoga practice, you might take advantage of the primacy effect by offering a dedication, such as "I dedicate this practice to my awakening so that I may be an instrument of Thy peace." As you finish your practice, you take advantage of the recency effect and repeat the dedication.

The same wisdom can be applied to the beginning and end of each day. It's also a good idea to craft some kind of ritual that signals the end of your work life and the beginning of your home life, especially if you are in a relationship. Taking a minute or two with your partner after work to honor your connection to each other, and to a higher purpose, can transform the hours you spend together, giving you a deeper sense of alignment with your beloved.

> "Whosoever would see how the soul dwells within its body let him observe how this body uses its daily habitation, for if this is without order and confused the body will be kept in disorder and confusion by its soul."
> —*Leonardo da Vinci*

CREATE A SPIRITUALLY NURTURING ENVIRONMENT

Your everyday environment serves as food for your soul. You can choose an exquisite feast or a spartan repast, but if you don't choose consciously, you're much more likely to get the spiritual equivalent of Spam, because spiritually nourishing influences aren't readily available in our commercially overloaded world.

Most of us live in a spiritually benumbing environment of billboards, beepers, cell phones, e-mail, cubicles, multitasking, traffic jams, security screening, artificial ingredients, jackhammers, and reality TV. Assaulted by so much visual and aural static, most of us find it all too easy, as Leonardo said, "to look without seeing."

Leonardo himself was careful to cultivate an environment that was aethetically pleasing, for he understood its role in creating inner harmony.

You can sharpen your spiritual *sensazione* and nurture your soul by creating a "habitation" that reflects and reminds you of the Divine. Here are a few simple things to do:

+ **Orchestrate your day.** In addition to being a skilled musician himself, Leonardo employed musicians to play for him while he worked in his studio. He understood that music can be used to facilitate creativity and well-being—effects that have been studied scientifically in our own time. For example, we now know that Mozart's music seems to have a positive energetic or "tuning" effect on sentient beings. In *The Mozart Effect* Don Campbell reports on research demonstrating the positive effects of Mozart's music on plant growth, milk production in cows, and intellectual performance in humans, among many other phenomena.

Many spiritual traditions have cultivated the use of sound to create the same positive tuning effect in order to promote healing, inner peace, and enlightenment.

Discover the music that you experience as most spiritually uplifting and "orchestrate" your day accordingly. (This book, for example, was written with a continuous loop of Gregorian chants playing in the background.)

✦ **Create an altar.** Dedicate a space in your home as a place of special focus on the Divine. Fill the space with objects and images that inspire you to remember your connection to something greater than your own ego. My altar is on the top of my dresser and currently displays photographs of my grandparents and parents, a plaque inscribed with the Prayer of St. Francis, an image of Leonardo's *Vitruvian Man,* a small sculpture of the Buddha, and an abstract painting of the opening of the heart chakra, along with other inspiring *memoria.*

✦ **Make scents.** Incense, fresh flowers, and essential oils are all delightful ways to enhance your inspiration and alter your consciousness. (I'm burning lavender incense and enjoying the sight and aroma of a bouquet of roses as I write—the lavender-rose combination was Leonardo's favorite aroma.)

✦ **Apply feng shui.** Feng shui is an ancient Chinese system for arranging rooms—placing mirrors, screens, fountains, and furniture—to balance the forces of yin and yang and maximize harmony with nature. It's like giving your home an acupuncture session. (Read Terah Kathryn Collins's excellent *The Western Guide to Feng Shui* to learn more.)

✦ **Touch energetically.** Imagine the quality of touch Leonardo brought to painting his angel. Deepak Chopra describes the underlying reality of this kind of touch: "If you choose, you can experience yourself in a state of unity with everything you contact. In ordinary . . . consciousness, you touch your finger to a rose and feel it as a solid, but in truth one bundle of energy and information—your finger—is contacting another bundle of energy and information—the rose." Leonardo's genius for spiritual *sensazione* allowed him to make this implicit order of energy and information manifest.

I've explored this quality of touch through my study of Leonardo, in classes on sensory awareness, and through thirty years of experience in the Alexander technique, but the most sensitive touch I've ever experienced is the pulse reading done by acupuncturist Lorie Dechar. I asked her to describe how she takes pulses to inspire you to take the pulse of your world:

Pulse reading plays a role in healing traditions the world over, and it is an important part of Chinese medical diagnosis. A skilled acupuncturist can determine the severity, depth, and organ location of disease by reading a patient's pulses. Sometimes it is even possible to determine how long a person has been sick and how soon they will recover.

There are twelve different pulse positions located bilaterally on the wrist, just above the radial artery. However, unlike the Western doctor, the acupuncturist palpates not the actual blood pulse of the artery but rather the reflected vibration of the pulse in the surrounding body tissue. When I explain pulse taking to patients, I describe the radial pulse as being like a stone thrown in a pond. As an acupuncturist, I am not interested in the stone itself, but rather the waves that ripple outward from the splash. These ripples give me information about the movements of the *qi* (*aka chi, prana, ki,* life force) and give me an inside view of the body, mind, and spirit of my patient.

When an acupuncturist takes a patient's pulse, she or he places the fingers on the wrist just above the artery and listens to the ripples with the tips of the fingers. At first, students learning pulse diagnosis usually claim to feel nothing. But with time and practice, their sensitivity to sensation develops and a whole new world opens up at their fingertips. Over time, the pulses can be read and then tuned the way a master musician tunes the strings of a guitar. Careful listening allows the acupuncturist to sometimes change off-key, twanging pulses into the harmonized chiming of a dozen golden bells.

TOP TEN SPIRITUAL PLAYLIST

Created with the help of musician and sound healing specialist Gene Jones, this playlist is designed to help you cultivate your spiritual *sensazione* through music.

1. *Chakra Chants*, Jonathan Goldman
   A healing journey from the base chakra through the crown.
2. *Sound Massage*, Brigitte Hamm
   Crystal bowls and voice. Pure magic!
3. *One Track Heart*, Krishna Das
   My favorite music for driving. Helps me to bless instead of curse those people who cut me off on the New Jersey Turnpike.
4. *Om*, Yoga International
   All om, all the time. Superb expression of this universal mantra.
5. *Chant Meditation*, Jade/BMG Music
   Gregorian chants: my favorite accompaniment for "getting into the zone" while writing.
6. *Harmonic Resonance*, Jim Oliver
   Very soothing, deep tones for meditation and contemplation.
7. *The Power of 7*, Brian E. Paulson
   Wonderful for opening the inner eye and harmonizing the heart.
8. *Everyday Ecstasy*, Margot Anand
   A celebration of passion, spirit, and joy.
9. *The Harmonic Choir: Hearing Solar Winds*, David Hykes
   Sounds of inner freedom.
10. *7 Metals*, Benjamin Iobst
    Gene Jones calls this the "finest Tibetan bowls CD available."

Addiction is rampant in our culture. Alcoholism, drug abuse, and overeating affect many families. But there's one addiction that affects all of us—the addiction to waiting. We wait for things to get better if they're not so good, or to go wrong if they are good. "So tired, tired of waiting, tired of waiting for yooo-ooo-oou" goes the old rock song. But even when we get whom or what we want, we seem never to stop waiting—waiting for things to be the way they used to be, waiting to have enough money or sex or fun or success, or waiting for enlightenment.

The Maestro knew about waiting:

> Behold now the hope or desire of going back to one's own country . . . like that of the moth to the light, of the man who with perpetual longing always looks forward with joy to each new spring and each new summer . . . deeming that the things he longs for are too slow in coming; and who does not perceive that he is longing for his own destruction.

Enlightenment is waiting for you to *stop waiting*!

At the funeral of the sage Rabbi Moshe, Rabbi Mendel asked one of his disciples: "What was most important to your teacher?" The disciple replied, "Whatever he happened to be doing at the moment."

—*Hasidic wisdom*

This Leonardo drawing is a remarkable evocation of reverent inner awareness. Leonardo extolled the virtue of taking time alone to relax, look, and listen within. You can cultivate your spiritual *sensazione* by experimenting with silence. Remaining silent, consciously, for an hour, a morning, or a whole day is a powerful practice for consolidating your energy and finding inner peace.

*E*ngage the Shadow (Sfumato)

> *If you bring forth what is within you, what*
> *you bring forth will save you. If you do not*
> *bring forth what is within you, what you do not*
> *bring forth will destroy you.*
>
> —GOSPEL OF THOMAS

St. John the Baptist was probably Leonardo's last complete oil painting; being the last, it inevitably leads us to speculate about his state of mind toward the end of his life.

When Leonardo died on May 2, 1519, at the Clos de Luce in Amboise, France, only three of his masterpieces remained in his possession, but they were among his very greatest: the *Mona Lisa, Virgin and Child with St. Anne,* and his most haunting work of all, *St. John the Baptist.* Although it is hard to pin down what gives this painting its unique power, we do know that certain quintessentially Leonardian techniques are partially responsible. The luminous intensity of St. John's androgynous image emerging out of an obscure darkness into golden light makes it one of the Maestro's most extraordinary demonstrations of the *sfumato* effect.

Sfumato, a word derived from the Latin root *fumus,* which means "smoky," is a term art critics coined to describe the hazy, mysterious quality that characterizes many of Leonardo's paintings. The *sfumato* effect achieved by Leonardo was perfectly complemented by another method he pioneered, *chiaroscuro*—the dramatic disposition of highlights and shadows. As Vasari described the result, "To the art of painting, he added a kind of shadowing to the method of colouring with oils which has enabled the moderns to endow their figures with great energy and relief."

But the effects Leonardo achieved were not simply examples of great technical mastery and ingenuity; they are intrinsic elements of the meaning and emotional power of his works. In this painting, Leonardo is going beyond his scientific observation of nature to a realm he called *termine* (boundary) or *essere di nulla* (being in the void). Leonardo asked: What is the boundary between water from a river and the water it meets as it enters the ocean? What is the nature of the place where a wave meets the air, where moonlight ultimately dissipates, or where something meets nothing? And how is it that heaven meets earth? These questions are alive in his representation of St. John the Baptist, the patron saint of Florence—the simple man who emerged from his thirty years in the desert wilderness to herald the coming of the Messiah ("The kingdom of heaven is at hand," Matthew 4:17; "I indeed baptize you with water; but there shall come one mightier than I," Luke 3:16). We can better appreciate the profundity of Leonardo's portrait if we recognize that he is using all his powers to push us beyond the boundaries of the known and the knowable.

As Kenneth Clark comments about Leonardo's evocation of St. John: "St. John the Baptist was the forerunner of the Truth and the Light. And what is the inevitable precursor of truth? A question. Leonardo's St. John is the eternal question mark, the enigma of creation."

If a question is, as Clark suggests, an inevitable precursor of truth, then what is the inevitable precursor of light?

Darkness.

Leonardo's painted figure emerges from darkness into light, as John emerged from the desert into the knowledge of the "word of the Lord," and his remarkable gesture seems to point the way to redemption. But Leonardo's St. John also taunts us with unabashed sensuality and a touch of salaciousness. Leonardo challenges us to reconcile the piety of the heavenly gesture with the spiraling bearskin on the naked body.

The face of Leonardo's St. John resembles both the St. John next to Christ in *The Last Supper* and his St. Anne, but with a smile whose ambiguity rivals that of the *Mona Lisa* and a strange, disturbing gaze—perhaps the look of a man who has glimpsed ultimate salvation as well as the more imminent reality of his own beheading. Many critics have described this spiraling, smiling pose and the uncanny relationship of light and darkness in this painting as the quintessence of Leonardo's ability to express eternal mystery.

Leonardo's search for light and truth through ceaseless questioning, his willingness to take responsibility for his own thoughts and ideas, and his ever-deepening understanding led him to many great insights and discoveries, but—as his disquieting St. John suggests—it also led him to confront the enigmatic realm of the shadows from which John emerged. This was a man who described caring tenderly for an old man who was dying, comforting him through his last breath—then dissecting him as soon as the pulse was gone. Leonardo had a curiosity about death that was as insatiable as his appetite for life, and in his description of the deathbed and dissection scene we see him attempting to learn the secrets of life by exploring the wake of death.

Leonardo wrote six books on the relationship of shadow and light. He discovered and described in detail the nature of the phenomenon of umbra, which is defined by Webster's dictionary as "the shadow from which all light from a given source is excluded by an object," and penumbra, "the partial shadow cast by a body where light from a given source is not wholly excluded." But as we see in his portrait of St. John, Leonardo's exploration of shadow wasn't just a technical exercise; it reflected his confrontation with the dark side of human nature, including his own.

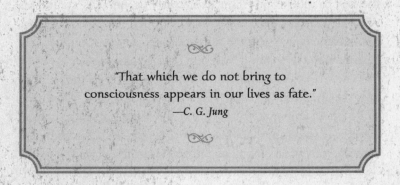

"That which we do not bring to
consciousness appears in our lives as fate."
—C. G. Jung

Psychiatrist C. G. Jung referred to the dark side of our being as the "shadow" and emphasized that by repressing, ignoring, or failing to understand it we increase its power. In his words, "Everyone carries a shadow, and the less it is embodied in the individual's conscious life . . . the denser it is. At all counts, it forms an unconscious snag, thwarting our most well-meant intentions."

Leonardo's many studies of the Deluge, the extraordinary contrasts in his St. John, and the frequent juxtapositioning of ugliness and beauty that occurs throughout his work, where images of battles and gruesome war machines can be found on the same page as beautiful flowers and sparkling streams of water, are all artistic expressions of his understanding that experience is many-faceted, almost too rich for human understanding. As Jung has said, "Life consists of a complex of inexorable opposites— day and night, birth and death, happiness and misery, good and evil. We are not even sure that one will prevail against the other, that good will overcome evil, or joy defeat pain."

Leonardo's confrontation with the tension of opposites on the spiritual level became increasingly profound throughout his career. The limitless optimism of his youth gave way later to expressions of self-doubt and despair.

The twisting and turning characteristic of the torsos he drew and painted seem to reflect the tension of his inner state. He writes over and over in the margins of his notebooks, "Have I really accomplished anything?" He witnesses and is touched by war, destruction, death, brutality, hypocrisy, and betrayal. He serves in the courts of shadowy characters such as Ludovico

CONTRAPOSTO

In addition to his innovative use of the techniques of *sfumato* and *chiaroscuro*, Leonardo also championed *contraposto* as a means of bringing more dynamic tension to his subjects. He describes it thus:

> Never make the head turn the same way as the torso, nor the arm and leg move together on the same side. And if the face is turned to the right shoulder, make all the parts lower in the left than on the right; and when you turn the body with the breast outwards, if the head turns to the left side make the parts on the right hand side higher than those on the left.

Sforza and the notorious Cesare Borgia. Leonardo seems at times to be reflecting the sentiments of his countryman Dante:

> Midway upon the journey of life
> I found myself within a forest dark,
> For the straightforward pathway had been lost . . .
> So bitter it is, death is little more.

Indeed, Leonardo seems to have experienced a crisis of confidence in his later years. The young genius who had written "The knowledge of all things is possible" discovered that there were some things beyond his capacity to know or understand. As he noted toward the end of his life, "Nature is full of infinite causes that experience has never demonstrated." And in a more personal expression, "While I thought I was learning how to live, I have been learning how to die."

Even great geniuses such as Leonardo are susceptible to doubt and darkness—to the play of the shadow side of the self. For Leonardo, this was evident in his reaction to the considerable jealousy and envy to which he was subject throughout his life. We don't have to psychoanalyze him to sense that he had trouble dealing with the feelings that arose from his sensitivity in this area. The comments he made about envy in his notebooks speak for themselves:

Envy wounds with false accusation.

The moment that virtue is born it gives birth to the envy it provokes: and a body may more readily be separated from its shadow than virtue from envy.

Envy: It is said of the kite that when it sees its nestlings grow too fat, it pecks their sides out of envy and leaves them without food.

Envy is represented making an obscene gesture towards heaven for, if she could, she would use her powers against God. . . .She wears a mask over her fair face. Her eye is wounded by the palm and the olive branch, her ear by the laurel and myrtle, for triumph and truth offend her. Lightning flashes from her to symbolize the wickedness of her language. She is gaunt and wrinkled, for perpetual desire consumes her; a fiery serpent gnaws at her heart. She carries a quiver with tongues for arrows, for she often wounds with the tongue. . . . She carries in her hands a vase of flowers in which lie concealed scorpions, toads, and other venomous beasts. She rides astride death, over which she triumphs, for she is immortal. . . . She is laden with diverse weapons, and all are weapons of destruction.

There is a tinge of paranoia in Leonardo's railings about envy, and perhaps something self-deceiving in the vehement condemnations of lies, ingratitude, violence, anger, and drunkenness that occur in so many places in his notebooks. At times he seems to be dismissing all of humanity: "Well have I known man and he is much against my liking. He is a receptacle of villainy; a perfect heap of the utmost ingratitude combined with every vice." But that kind of blanket condemnation implicates the writer, too.

Leonardo's struggles remind us of his humanity, his fallibility, and they highlight the most overlooked and perhaps most important element of the spiritual journey—the need to engage the shadow side of our nature so that we don't act it out.

Why do so many gurus get caught embezzling? Why are so many priests charged with child abuse? Why do so many true believers commit torture and murder in the name of their god? And do all of us hold these same dark impulses in the basements and attics of our being?

The shadow is dangerous when it lurks in the unconscious. And many people who identify themselves with the desire for good and for God ignore or suppress their inner demons. We all have those demons within us. But all too often we do not recognize or acknowledge them because they are uncomfortable to confront, so they remain submerged until they leak out as spite, judgment, passive aggression, or worse.

Jung frames this most difficult challenge to the spiritual seeker in these poetic words:

> That I feed the hungry, that I forgive an insult, that I love my enemy in the name of Christ—all these are undoubtedly great virtues. What I do unto the least of my brethren, that I do unto Christ. But what if I should discover that the least among them all, the poorest of all the beggars, the most impudent of all offenders, the very enemy himself—that these are within me, and that I myself stand in need of the alms of my own kindness—that I myself am the enemy who must be loved—what then?

As though speaking in direct response to the challenge posed by Jung, the Sufi poet Jalaluddin Rumi offers this moving reflection on the many selves within us:

> This being human is a guest-house.
> Every morning a new arrival.
> A joy, a depression, a meanness,
> some momentary awareness comes
> as an unexpected visitor.
> Welcome and entertain them all!
> Even if they're a crowd of sorrows,
> who violently sweep your house
> empty of its furniture,
> still, treat each guest honorably.
> He may be cleaning you out
> for some new delight.
> The dark thought, the shame, the malice,
> meet them at the door laughing,
> and invite them in.
> Be grateful for whoever comes,
> because each has been sent
> as a guide from beyond.

Engaging the shadow, inviting in the shame and malice with gratitude, and taking responsibility for our dark thoughts and meanness yields, paradoxically, more true calm and peace than endless hours of meditation. Until we engage the shadow we are always running from it, denying it, and the more we run away and deny this aspect of ourselves, the more powerful and dangerous it becomes.

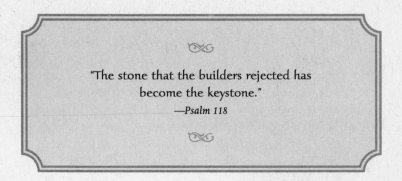

"The stone that the builders rejected has become the keystone."
—*Psalm 118*

Dr. Connie Zweig is a psychotherapist and a pioneer in guiding people to engage the shadow. With her collaborators Steve Wolf and Jeremiah Abrams, she coined the term *shadow-work* to describe the process of cultivating a creative engagement with the dark side of the self.

She describes the benefits of the process in *Meeting the Shadow*:

+ Achieving a more genuine self-acceptance, based on a more complete knowledge of who we are
+ Defusing the negative emotions that erupt unexpectedly in our daily lives
+ Feeling freer of the guilt and shame associated with our negative feelings and actions
+ Recognizing the projections that color our opinion of others
+ Healing our relationships through more honest self-examination and direct communication
+ Using the creative imagination via dreams, drawing, writing, and rituals to own the disowned self

THE PATH OF SHADOW-WORK

Zweig and Wolf advise, "Shadow awareness is not an easy path, a road on which the debris has been cleared and the direction lies straight ahead. Rather, to live with shadow awareness we follow the detours; we walk into the debris, groping our way through dark corridors and past dead ends." They counsel that rather than confronting the shadow as a problem to be solved or "cured," we relate to it as a mystery to be explored.

They explain that the work of shadow awareness requires us to:

+ Take responsibility
+ Stop blaming others
+ Move slowly
+ Deepen awareness
+ Sacrifice our ideals of perfection
+ Embrace paradox
+ Open our hearts

"Leonardo's struggle with the shadow is apparent in his life and work," comments Dr. Zweig. "I'm particularly struck by Vasari's observation that his shadowing technique enabled later artists to 'endow their figures with great energy and relief.' A creative relationship to the shadow within also yields 'great energy and relief.'"

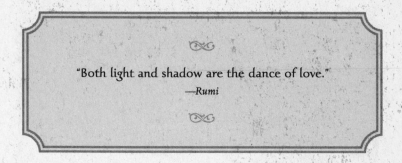

"Both light and shadow are the dance of love."
—*Rumi*

Leonardo groped his way through dark corridors that often led to dead ends; he willingly walked into the unknown; and always, no matter how great the darkness, he persevered in his quest for truth. And we sense that he discovered something transformative in his confrontation with the shadow. Despite sometimes feeling alone and wounded, he always continued, reminding us that our blackest moments may herald new light.

Just as Leonardo's smiling St. John emerges out of the darkness to point the way to truth and light, so our own engagement with the mysteries of the shadow can enlighten us. This spiritual aspect of shadow work is expressed most exquisitely by Jorge Luis Borges:

> From the tireless labyrinth of dreams I returned as if to my home, to the harsh prison. I blessed its dampness, I blessed its tiger, I blessed the crevice of light. I blessed my old, suffering body. I blessed the darkness and the stone. Then there occurred what I cannot forget or communicate. There occurred the union with the divinity, with the universe.

Engage the Shadow: Self-Assessment

✎

☐ I'm aware of my feelings of anger.

☐ I'm aware of my feelings of greed.

☐ I'm aware of my feelings of envy and jealousy.

☐ I'm aware of my anxieties and fears.

☐ Sometimes my words and actions express spite or contempt.

☐ Sometimes my words and actions express greed and covetousness.

☐ Sometimes my words and actions express envy and jealousy.

☐ Sometimes my words or actions express anxiety and fear.

☐ I recognize the evil, pain, and suffering in the world.

☐ I am aware of the way in which my criticisms, judgments, and anger toward others reflect my own weaknesses.

⚜ Engage the Shadow: Spiritual Practices

"Perhaps all the dragons of our lives are princesses who are only waiting to see us once beautiful and brave. Perhaps everything terrible is in its deepest being something helpless that wants help from us."

—RAINER MARIA RILKE

ME AND MY SHADOW: INVITING AWARENESS

"Are you aware of your unconscious expressions of hostility toward this panel?" That's the question posed to Robert De Niro's character by the head of the mental hospital in which he is confined in the movie *Awakenings*. De Niro replies, "If they're unconscious, how could I be aware of them?"

The shadow is, by definition, unconscious. Before we can engage it creatively and channel its powerful energy in more positive directions, we must know that it exists and begin to recognize its manifestations. Please reflect on the following clues for shadow recognition and record examples from your own experience in your notebook. You can recognize the presence of the shadow in:

+ Hypercritical reactions to others; exaggerated, dismissive judgments
+ Sneaky feelings of superiority, envy, self-righteousness, and greed
+ Reactions of extreme defensiveness to critical feedback from others (especially when you find that you are getting similar feedback from several different people)

- ✦ "Unintentional," impulsive statements and actions
- ✦ A repeated pattern of actions that cause you shame and humiliation
- ✦ Passive-aggressive behavior

MAPPING YOUR SHADOW

Leonardo created amazingly accurate maps of towns in central Italy for his shadowy patron Cesare Borgia. And he also drew remarkably precise and descriptive expressions of the relationship between light and shadow. Kenneth Clark points out: "It is often said that Leonardo drew so well because he knew about things; it is truer to say that he knew about things because he drew so well."

The exploration of your inner shadow doesn't require the drawing prowess of a Leonardo, but you can learn more about this aspect of yourself by exploring it through drawing.

Prepare by opening to a blank page in your notebook or by placing a large sheet of blank white paper on a table, desk, or easel. Choose a few different colored pens, pencils, or markers, or if you prefer, you can use pastels or plain black charcoal.

Enjoy a few deep, sighing exhalations, and then take a minute or two to sit quietly and just follow the flow of your breathing.

Then imagine that you are walking on a beautiful path through piney woods on a perfect, sunny day. You feel a deep sense of safety, connectedness, and belonging as you stroll along. As you walk along, you listen to the sound of each footstep and feel the pine needles underfoot. A golden, protective light surrounds you as you enjoy the dappled sunlight coming through the trees and the invigorating aroma of pine and earth. With every step you take you allow yourself to feel more connected with the beauty around and within you.

As you look ahead you see a fork in the path, and standing at the vertex of the fork is someone that you wish wasn't there, blocking your way. It could be an actual person from your life now or in the past, a historical figure, or a composite being who represents everything you detest, someone who seems to embody the opposite of the beauty you are experiencing. Take as much time as you need to visualize this unwelcome intruder. Notice the size, facial features, and body type as well as the demeanor, expression, and attitude.

Then listen as the intruder speaks to you, paying attention to both the words and the tone of voice. What does the ogre say? What's the quality of the voice tone? How does this make you feel? Angry? Disgusted? Contemptuous? Frightened? Aroused? What is it that particularly offends you?

Now, begin drawing the images, shapes, and colors that your shadow figure evokes. Avoid editing or judging what you draw. Just let it go. Fill your page(s) with as many impressions as you can. Your drawing can be purely abstract or representational, or you can go back and forth between these two modes. In any case, just let your drawing emerge from the feelings that your shadow figure provokes. Don't attempt to analyze your drawings or yourself; just keep drawing.

When you feel that you have drawn enough, take a break. You may find that you feel energized from this simple practice. You may also feel heightened anxiety. In any case, take a break, let go of the shadow-mapping exercise completely, and take a brisk walk or engage in some other form of physical activity.

When you're ready, go back to your drawings. Choose the one that seems to have the most energy and redraw it in the center of another blank sheet of paper. Then, on lines flowing out from your central image, print key words and draw other images that you associate with your central image. Again, avoid editing or analyzing at this stage and just free-associate with your central image. After you've filled the page with images and key word associations, step back and look at your shadow map, and ask yourself:

- What are the parts of myself that I may have disowned?
- How could I become more receptive to the messages that my shadow holds for me?
- If my shadow has a message for me, what would it be?
- What aspects of my shadow figure can I recognize in myself?
- If my shadow did a drawing of me, what would it look like?

Mapping your shadow in this way may help to bring some of the disowned parts of your psyche to the surface. Representing these repressed elements of the self on paper makes it easier to engage the shadow in a relatively objective and less threatening way.

HIT A PILLOW

While painting and drawing are effective ways of allowing a catharsis and transformation of these shadow elements, physical enactments, such as martial arts practices or the practice below, can also be therapeutic.

In the movie *Analyze This*, Billy Crystal plays a hapless therapist who finds himself treating a Mafia boss played by Robert De Niro. De Niro's character suffers from panic attacks followed by fits of anger and rage. Crystal explains that when he gets angry he "hits a pillow," and he suggests that his client do the same. De Niro immediately whips out his .45 and pumps slugs into the pillow on the couch. Crystal asks sheepishly, "Feel better?" And De Niro replies, "Yeah, I do."

Although frequently satirized and much misunderstood, this simple method can serve as an effective tool for venting feelings of anger, spite, and rage.

Some guidelines for doing it safely and effectively:

+ Don't use a .45.
+ Do it in private.
+ Choose something to hit that safely absorbs your impact without damage to it or you—a mattress, a pillow, etc.
+ Get out an old tennis racket to use instead of your fists.
+ Imagine that the object that you are striking is the object of your enmity.
+ Keep your eyes open and in contact with the object you are striking.
+ Breathe fully throughout the exercise. Do not hold your breath.
+ Yell and scream as you strike. Feel free to use expletives.

You can achieve the same benefits by lying in bed on your back and kicking and punching the mattress.

When you exhaust yourself from this cathartic practice, take some time to just relax and breathe. You may find that as you burn through rage and spite, you feel sadness underneath; allow yourself to feel it. You may also find that energy is now flowing more freely through your body. Allow yourself to feel that, too.

Avoid judging yourself for whatever negative feelings arise or for whatever unpleasant sentiments you express when you vocalize. It's much better to take these out on your mattress or pillow than on others or yourself.

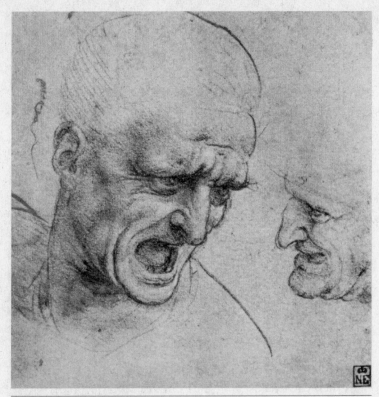

According to Professor Martin Kemp, this sketch for Leonardo's *Battle of Anghiari* is probably based on the face of the Milanese mercenary Niccolò Piccinino. Leonardo aims to capture the moment when Florentine forces wrench the battle standard from Piccinino's hands. As Kemp describes it, "His face is contorted with rage, his brows gathered into deep furrows and his gap-toothed mouth is torn open to its maximum extension."

Giorgio Vasari describes the painting for which this sketch was made as the quintessence of "fury, hate and rage." Along with Goya's *Tres de Mayo* and Picasso's *Guernica*, Leonardo's *Battle of Anghiari* stands as one of the most powerful representations of brutality, terror, and violence in the history of art.

Though these are extreme representations, they depict dark forces that lurk within all of us. Anyone who can portray them with as much power and persuasiveness as these artists have done has to be in touch with his or her own dark forces, demons, or shadows—call them what you will.

CHAPTER 9

Cultivate Balance (Arte/Scienza)

The Mysterious Feminine never dies . . .
although She becomes the whole universe.
Her immaculate purity is never lost.
Although She assumes countless forms
Her true identity remains intact.
Tao is limitless, unborn, eternal—
It can only be reached through
the Mysterious Feminine.
She is the very face of the Absolute.

—LAO-TZU

The *Mona Lisa* is Leonardo's supreme evocation of the balance of masculine and feminine principles.

In 1999 the Rappahannock County, Virginia, school district sponsored a three-hour class on "How to Think Like Leonardo da Vinci" for eighty gifted children, ages eight to eleven. When the children were presented with the *Mona Lisa* and asked, "What is she smiling about?" they began immediately to imitate her

How to Smile Like Mona Lisa

"Close the mouth at the right corner with a suave
and nimble movement, and open it at the left side,
as if you were smiling secretly . . . not in an
artificial manner, but as though unconsciously—this is
not affectation, if it is done in moderation and
in a restrained and graceful manner and
accompanied by innocent coquetry and
certain movements of the eyes."
—*Advice for noble women in Agnolo Firenzuola's* Della perfetta
bellezza d'una donna *(Of the perfect beauty of a woman), 1541*

pose and smile, trying to discover the answer through reenact-
ment. (Please try this now as you continue to read so that you too
can experience the inner shift that occurs as you adopt this expression.) After a few moments a girl sitting in the back of the room
raised her hand and said: "She's got a secret." And then a boy in the
front blurted out: "She knows that everything has a opposite!" And
then another child added: "Yeah, just like boys and girls."

As the gifted boys and girls understood, Mona Lisa is the
high priestess of what Jung called the *mysterium coniunctionis*, the
inner marriage of masculine and feminine energies. Her smile is
Leonardo's magical expression of the timeless dance of yin and
yang, the totality of nature and human experience.

In his classic *The Renaissance*, Walter Pater offers a description
of *Mona Lisa* as "this beauty, into which the soul with all its mal-
adies has passed." Brimming with images of rebirth and reincar-

nation, his text helps us gain access to the profound spiritual insight that makes her portrait such a great painting:

> All the thoughts and experience of the world have etched and moulded there . . . the animalism of Greece, the lust of Rome, the mysticism of the middle ages . . . the return of the pagan world, the sins of the Borgias. She is older than the rocks among which she sits . . . she had been dead many times, and learned the secrets of the grave; and has been a diver in deep seas . . . and trafficked for strange webs with Eastern merchants, and, as Leda, was the mother of Helen of Troy, and as Saint Anne, the mother of Mary; and all this has been to her but as the sound of lyres and flutes.

How did Leonardo achieve this miraculous effect? The *Mona Lisa,* his supreme evocation of the balance of masculine and feminine principles, emerged from his marriage of art and science, *arte/scienza.* Both the bewitching face, which seems, as Vasari first noted, to be "real flesh rather than paint," and the fantastic mountains, flowing water, and beguiling atmospheric effects in the background were born from endless hours of anatomical, botanical, climatological, geometrical, and perspectival study wed to numinous intuitions, imagination, dreams—and a touch of magic.

For the figure in the *Mona Lisa,* whomever she may be based on, Leonardo drew not just on his great technical skill and his knowledge of anatomy, but on the ample resources of his *fantasia.* Although he may or may not have ever portrayed Eve—according to Vasari, he did create a cartoon of Adam and Eve, depicting them "in a meadow with an infinite number of flowers"—we sense that he intended the figure in the *Mona Lisa* to be a reincarnation of Eve, framed as she is in a background that is Eden-like in its tender, perfect luminescence. The core of our creation story, the story of paradise, is a metaphor for the need to balance and integrate the masculine and feminine principles.

MATHEMATICS AND *FANTASIA*: WHY IS THE SKY BLUE?

Leonardo's stature as perhaps the greatest genius in human history is predicated on his unparalleled balance of art and science. He applied the masculine principle in his rigorous, detailed analysis of the world around him, and the feminine principle in his love of nature, his deep feeling for his subjects, and his playful, unfettered imagination. Leonardo counseled his students to muse on abstract forms such as clouds or smoke in order to stimulate their *fantasia* (his word for "imagination") and also to be mathematically precise—"no human investigation," he noted, "can be called true science without going through mathematical tests." We can see the balance of these two principles reflected throughout his works, and in the notes he wrote giving an answer to the question many a child has asked: Why is the sky blue? "I say that the blue which is seen in the atmosphere is not its own colour but is caused by warm humidity evaporated in minute and imperceptible atoms on which the solar rays fall rendering them luminous against the immense darkness." Leonardo's superb powers of observation are the source of his ability to create the rich atmospherics that give the *Mona Lisa* its mystery and its magic.

We all emerge from a source of pure potentiality, the Garden of Eden, and we all have as our birthright both the masculine (Adam) and feminine (Eve) principles. Balancing these energies within allows us to return to the Garden—a truth that has been intuited by traditions as diverse as yoga, Taoism, and psychotherapy, particularly in the work of Carl Jung.

Jung referred to the masculine principle as the *animus* and the feminine principle as the *anima*. In his view the path to individuation demanded the "inner marriage" of these psychic principles, which was a task even more challenging than engaging with the shadow. In fact, he called shadow work the "apprentice-piece" on the path to wholeness, while the balancing and harmonizing of male-female energies was the "master-piece." Leonardo's *Mona Lisa* is a masterpiece of painting that seems to represent this masterpiece of inner work.

My friend Michael Frederick has focused on methods of inner work, including an intensive study of yoga with great masters such as J. Krishnamurti and T. K. Desikachar, for more than thirty years. Commenting on Leonardo's delicate feat of psychic balance, he says, "Although the legends of Leonardo traveling to the East don't appear to have a basis in fact, he seems nevertheless to have understood and expressed the essence of Yogic philosophy. The ideal of masculine/feminine balance is at the heart of Yoga practice."

Yogic science posits that the human body is home to seventy-two thousand *nadis*, subtle streams through which the energy of life, called *prana*, flows. These streams merge in the *susumna*, a central river of *prana* coursing through the full length of the spinal column. The *susumna* has two complementary currents. The right current conveys the active, hot, dry, male energy and is called the *surya nadi* (*surya* translates as "sun"). The left current conveys the passive, cool, wet, female energy and is called *chandra nadi* (*chandra* translates as "moon"). As renowned consciousness researcher and author of *The Way of the Mystic* Dr. Joan Borysenko points out:

The balance of these energies is thought to be critical for health, well-being, creativity and God-union. When the male and female energies come to balance, the latent energy at the base of the spine, called kundalini, shoots up the susumna, opens the chakras, and delivers the individual to God-Union, which is the actual meaning of Yoga.

Similarly, in the ancient tradition of Taoism, achieving a harmonious interplay between yin, the female principle, and yang, the male principle, is the essential secret of personal enlightenment and societal harmony.

As Lao-tzu writes in the *Tao-te Ching*:

> All things have their back to the female
> And stand facing the male.
> When male and female combine
> All things achieve harmony.

The balancing of male and female, front and back, yin and yang, is also the basis of the Chinese healing arts. Lori Dechar is an acupuncturist and professor at Tri-State College of Acupuncture in New York City. She is the author of *Five Spirits: The Alchemical Mystery at the Heart of Traditional Chinese Medicine*, and, as I can testify from firsthand experience, a remarkably gifted healer.

Early in her career Dechar felt that there was a limitation in the way that acupuncture was being taught. As she explains: "The discovery of acupuncture is usually attributed to the first great leader of China, Huang Di, the legendary Yellow Emperor. However, according to myth, Huang Di was actually the consort of Xi Wang Mu, the Queen Mother of the West, none other than the Earth Goddess herself; and it was from the goddess that the emperor gained the gift of wisdom and healing power." Dechar intuited that at some point in its evolution the literature and teaching methods of Chinese medicine had been hijacked by a patriarchal power play: "This distortion has led to a neglect of the roots of the tradition: its devotion to the feminine, matter and the Earth and especially, the embodied soul as the yin reflection of yang spirit. Lao Tzu reminds us over and over again of the crucial importance of the balancing of yin and yang."

Seeking to correct this distortion, Dechar learned to interpret Chinese characters so that she could go back to ancient Chinese medical texts and Taoist writings and gain an unfettered understanding of her art. She discovered that many of Chinese medicine's original teachings were based on the principles of Taoist alchemy, an ancient spiritual discipline and natural science that honors the crucial importance of feminine wisdom in healing and spiritual transformation. According to the Taoist alchemical tradition, spirit—the invisible yang energy of the Divine—is not waiting to be discovered after death, high up and far away in heaven. Rather, the Divine is present, here and now, interpenetrating the world of matter and our daily lives on earth. Spirit is invisible, yet it can be seen through its yin manifestation in the cycles, movements, and forms of the natural world.

Dechar's studies also revealed that many of the great Taoist teachers and healers of ancient China were women. She incorporated many of their practices into her work and found that these techniques greatly enhanced her ability to help her patients.

Dechar adds, "Leonardo was a Taoist. He reminds us, through his reverent and remarkably accurate evocations of the natural world, through Mona Lisa's smile and the androgyny of so many of his figures, that the inner marriage of masculine and feminine energies—the balance of yin and yang—can give birth to infinite worlds of the spirit and the rediscovery of paradise on earth."

> "The seed of the mother has the power
> in the embryo equally with
> that of the father."
> —*Leonardo da Vinci*

Cultivate Balance: Self-Assessment

- ☐ I am patient, receptive, and a good listener.
- ☐ I am in touch with the feminine principle inside myself.
- ☐ I am bold and assertive and know how to take the initiative.
- ☐ I am in touch with the masculine principle inside myself.
- ☐ I can move freely from patience and receptivity to bold action and vice versa.
- ☐ I experience a sense of harmony between the masculine and feminine aspects of my being.
- ☐ I appreciate the tension of the opposites.
- ☐ If I determined a ratio of feminine to masculine energy in myself, what would it be (e.g., 60/40, 80/20, etc.)?

⚛ Cultivate Balance: Spiritual Practices

SUN AND MOON BREATHING PRACTICE

This basic yogic breathing practice (*pranayama*) is designed to balance the two hemispheres of the cerebral cortex and harmonize the nervous system. On a subtler level, it is intended to bring about a union of the male and female energies.

According to yogic science, the right nostril is the conduit of the solar, or masculine, energy (breathing through the right nostril stimulates the left hemisphere). The left nostril relates to our lunar or feminine aspect (breathing through the left nostril stimulates the right hemisphere).

Sit comfortably with your spine upright and your palms resting easily on your thighs. Your eyes can be gently closed. Place the thumb of your right hand on the side of your right nostril, closing off the air passageway. Inhale through the left nostril for a slow count of four. Then, with the last two fingers of the right hand, close off the left nostril, so that both nostrils are closed, and retain the breath for another slow count of four. Release the thumb and breathe out through the right nostril for a slow count of eight. Next, breathe in through the right nostril for the count of four, close off the right nostril with the thumb so that both nostrils are closed, and hold for four counts. Release the fingers from the left nostril and slowly exhale on a count of eight from the left nostril. This is one complete cycle of sun and moon pranayama.

Do seven complete cycles and then when you are finished, let both hands rest on your thighs and focus on breathing slowly and evenly through both nostrils, with the intention of allowing the male and female energies within to come into balance.

Follow the flow of your breath all the way up both your nostrils to the point inside the head where the two nostrils join. When you find it you will have arrived at the place where male and female energies merge into pure consciousness. Rest in that place as your breath continues.

"Through your loving
Existence and non-existence merge.
All opposites unite.
All that is profane
Becomes sacred again."
—*Rumi*

FIVE-SPIRITS MEDITATION: BALANCING YIN AND YANG

The Five Spirits can be understood as the Taoist version of the chakra system of Vedic India. Like the chakras, the spirits exist as centers of consciousness in the subtle body rather than as structures in the physical body. The chakras and Five Spirits both function to balance the yang and yin aspects of our being and are based on the recognition of the inherent divinity of both feminine (earth) and masculine (heaven) energies. Unlike the chakras, however, which are visualized as abstract wheels of swirling energy, the Five Spirits are thought of as animating deities who reside in us, each with its own nature and psychospiritual function. An understanding of the Five Spirits is the key that opens the doorway to the mysteries of Taoist psychospiritual practice.

For this meditation, you may sit in a chair or on a cushion on the floor. What matters is simply that your back is straight, forming a vertical axis between the top of the head and the bottom of the tailbone.

Begin the meditation by visualizing your body as a mountain, your peak reaching up to heaven and your base planted deep in the earth. Take a moment to visualize your "mountain." Feel its beauty and power. Now, bring your awareness to the top of the head, the highest point of the mountain peak, the realm of the king of the eastern sky and the emperor of the rising sun. Visualize a single star shining just a few inches above your head. Feel the light of this star pouring down on you in a radiant shower of liquid gold. This is the light of the *shen* spirit, the yang light of heaven and conscious awareness.

Feel the golden light of the *shen* drift down through your body, coming to rest in the space at the center of your heart. As you breathe into the heart space, visualize the *shen* spirit taking on form and color, drifting and changing like the mists and clouds on the mountainside. As the yang light of awareness grows moister and more yin, we enter the realm of the *hun*, the spirit of vision and imagination.

Follow the light as it drifts downward, coming to rest in the solar plexus. As you breathe in to the solar plexus, feel the light gathering potency and weight as it descends toward earth. Feel the light take root in your belly like a seed taking root in the fertile valley at the mountain's edge. This is the realm of the *yi*, the spirit of embodied action and intention.

As your awareness moves down, it dips below the horizon, down into the dark caves below the mountain, down into the labyrinth of the viscera of the pelvic basin. Bring your awareness to a point about three inches below your navel and take a moment to feel the powerful energies that reside there. This is the realm of the *po*, the yin spirit of the animal body, the breath, and the autonomic nervous system.

Now, go deeper as your awareness follows the labyrinths of the viscera deep below the mountain, down to the darkest cave, down to a point at the base of the spine. Feel the energies that pulsate there, ebbing and flowing, as the tide of the cerebrospinal fluid rises and falls. Feel the darkness envelop you as the yang light of consciousness is swallowed in the dark ocean of the yin fluids of life. This is the realm of the *zhi*, the spirit of the collective unconscious, the spirit of archetypes, cell memories, genetic codes, primal symbols, and the luminous threads of fate that are the yin reflection of the Tao.

In the darkest cavern below the mountain, at the base of the spine, we come to the cinnabar throne of Xi Wang Mu, queen mother of the west, earth goddess of the divine instinctual body. Here we have reached the center of the transformational mystery, the dark womb of the mysterious feminine. Now, breathe and wait and do nothing. Surrender to her power. As you breathe down into the deepest, most hidden point of the body, you will gradually feel a tingling begin at the base of the spinal column. This tingling is the fire of the yin, the light that rises from down below, the fiery spring of the life force, the river of liquid light that gushes up from the heart of darkness.

Breathe this underworld fire upward, up through the pelvis and the solar plexus. When it reaches the heart, feel the luminous yin fire of the *zhi* spirit mingle with the radiant yang light of the *shen*. As you breathe in to the heart, feel the light pour in from above and below. As upper and lower lights mingle, you will feel subtle streams of pleasure radiate from the heart and fill your entire body. Compassion and love pour through you as you continue to breathe the two lights into your heart. You are now experiencing the sacred union, the marriage of yin and yang. Let the dance of this union continue as you open your eyes, and let the light of the spirits shine from your heart outward to the world.

WALK A LABYRINTH

Leonardo loved spiraling shapes and labyrinthine designs such as the ones he painted in the Sala delle Asse in the Sforza Castle. Walking a labyrinth is a simple, delightful way to center yourself as you cultivate the balance of masculine and feminine energies. The labyrinth is a single circuitous path, with one entrance leading to a central sanctuary and one exit. It isn't a maze or problem to be solved. Unlike a maze, there are no decision points, tricks, or cul-de-sacs. The path winds around itself but is easy to follow. In other words, you can't get it wrong or right—you just do it. And as you walk, you may find yourself releasing your attachment to internal opposition and instead "just being."

The labyrinth pattern is present in many cultures and traditions, dating back more than four thousand years. Perhaps the most famous example is at the amazing Chartres Cathedral in France. Inlaid in the stone floor in 1201, the Chartres labyrinth had fallen into disuse for more than two centuries until the Reverend Dr. Lauren Artress, canon for special ministry at Grace Cathedral in San Francisco, led a successful effort to reopen the Chartres labyrinth to the public and revive its function as a tool for meditation, prayer, and the cultivation of balance.

Artress created a replica of the Chartres labyrinth at Grace Cathedral, and through the organization she founded, called Veriditas, has promoted a global renaissance of this nondenominational celebration of inner peace and balance.

Labyrinths are now appearing in parks, cemeteries, prisons, schools, universities, hospitals, retreat centers, spas, and backyards. See if you can find one in your area. You may dedicate your labyrinth walk to a particular purpose, such as cultivating balance and healing, seeking creative inspiration, or offering a prayer of gratitude and celebration. The walk can be viewed as a three-part process: entering, centering, and integrating. In other words, you hold your question or purpose in your mind and heart as you enter. Once in the center, you touch the center of your own being, listening deeply for the wisdom within. Then, when you're ready, you walk out, preparing to integrate what you've received.

Or you can just stroll along without a formal question or purpose, as I did when I first tried it. (My first labyrinth walk took place at Rancho La Puerta in Tecate, Mexico, during the first week of working on this book. As I entered the center, I started to whirl spontaneously, like the Mevlevi dervishes I'd last seen in performance more than twenty-five years earlier. I felt the energy of light from above flowing through my heart and streaming down through my feet, connecting me more deeply with the earth. As I walked out I felt a deep sense of gratitude, realizing that I'd been given just what was needed for the completion of the task.) In any case, just find your own natural pace and listen to your heart with each step. If you like, you can bring your notebook and record your impressions along the way or upon completion.

How can we account for the balancing, healing, and harmonizing effects of this simple practice? Perhaps it's just the feeling of freedom that emerges from doing something that doesn't involve the pressure of right or wrong. Maybe the turning movements balance the two hemispheres of the cerebral cortex. Many labyrinth walkers intuit that walking the path serves as a metaphor for the spiritual journey of our lives. Artress comments, "Labyrinth-walking involves gently turning left, right, left, right and . . . somehow this balances and gives a sense of peace—almost like being rocked in a cradle."

You can find more than eighteen hundred labyrinth locations at wwll.veriditas.labyrinthsociety.org.

THE UNIVERSAL WISDOM
OF THE TAO

The yang, or masculine, principle manifests in planning and taking action. It is the mode for getting things done, for doing. Yang energy drives the process of setting goals. The masculine principle leads the effort to craft and implement strategies to fulfill our goals. Its shape is triangular.

The yin, or feminine, principle manifests in just being. Yin energy nurtures listening and receptivity and allows goals to come to completion. The feminine source of spacious stillness is the place from which all things arise. Its shape is circular.

Action emerges from nonaction, thought from nothought, doing from being, everything from nothing. The triangle enters the circle, the eternal spiral springs forth, Mona Lisa smiles.

As I write I'm looking at the mist floating above the Hudson River. I sense in my legs the gentle ripples I see on the surface of the water. Yang inhales for me, and yin releases my breath. Thank God for both (and thank both for God).

The Tao is apparent in nature, on the river, in the woods, on top of a mountain. But how do we remember it in the office or in traffic? Imitate Mona Lisa's smile. Bring your awareness to the flow of your breathing. And invoke the immortal words of Frank Zappa: "In the fight between you and the universe, back the universe."

In the 1980s men's groups, many inspired by Robert Bly's *Iron John,* formed to assert the value of the masculine principle and support men in feeling good about themselves in the face of dramatically changing expectations from women. Although some groups continue, the phenomenon has largely petered out. Meantime, women have been meeting to support one another in ever-increasing numbers in many formats, the most prolific of which is the book club.

My women friends who participate in these groups usually choose books that are the literary equivalent of "chick flicks." (A significant other once brought home a subtitled foreign-language film from this genre. When she left the room for a moment, I quickly fast-forwarded the video, attempting to find some action, but she caught me and asked: "What do you think you're doing?" "Speed reading," I replied.) As an author, wherever I go I'm always looking at what people are reading. I've never seen a man on an airplane reading *The Divine Secrets of the Ya-Ya Sisterhood,* and it is unusual to see a woman at the beach immersed in Tom Clancy.

A simple proposal for promoting a deeper understanding and balance of masculine and feminine energies and attitudes is to form a book club and alternate selections that are more popular with the two genders, respectively. A few suggestions are offered here, but these are meant just to inspire you to make choices of your own.

YIN READING LIST
Goddess in Every Woman, Jean Shinoda Bolen
A Room of One's Own, Virginia Woolf
Wild Mind, Natalie Goldberg
The Bean Trees, Barbara Kingsolver

A PERSONAL REFLECTION ON THE TAO

When I was thirty-five years old I set very clear, ambitious goals to be achieved in time for my fortieth birthday. They all came true. When I was forty I developed another five-year plan, and again, everything happened just as I visualized. Then at age forty-five I framed specific goals that I wished to achieve for my fiftieth birthday . . . and none of them were realized. At first I was upset, even depressed, particularly since I prided myself on helping individuals and organizations define, plan, and realize their goals.

But then I asked, "What's the underlying purpose of each goal?" The answer was clear, and humiliating in a liberating way: the underlying purpose was to feel connected, to experience deeper love and joy.

The next question was obvious: "Is it possible to feel connected, to experience deeper love and joy without the achievement of my goals?" In a blinding flash of the obvious I realized that of course it was, and that ironically, my intense focus on goal achievement may have actually been obscuring the real purpose of the goals. I surrendered to the tao of the situation. I didn't give up my pursuit of the goals but reframed the way I perceived them through the lens of my primary wish to experience love and connection—a wish that can come true every moment.

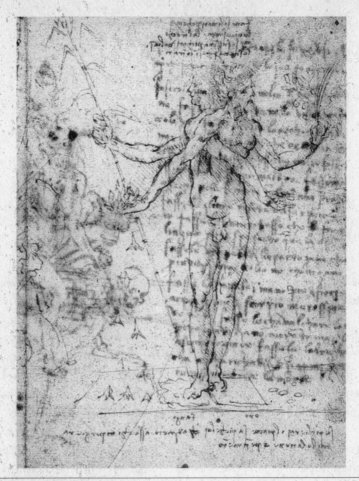

Leonardo didn't just recognize opposites; he understood the dynamic, paradoxical relationship between them, as we can see in his commentary on his drawing *The Allegory of Pleasure and Pain:* "Pleasure and Pain are shown as if they were twins . . . they are represented back to back, as if opposed to each other, but springing from a common trunk because they have one and the same foundation, for fatigue and pain are the foundation of pleasure, and vain and lascivious pleasures the foundation of pain."

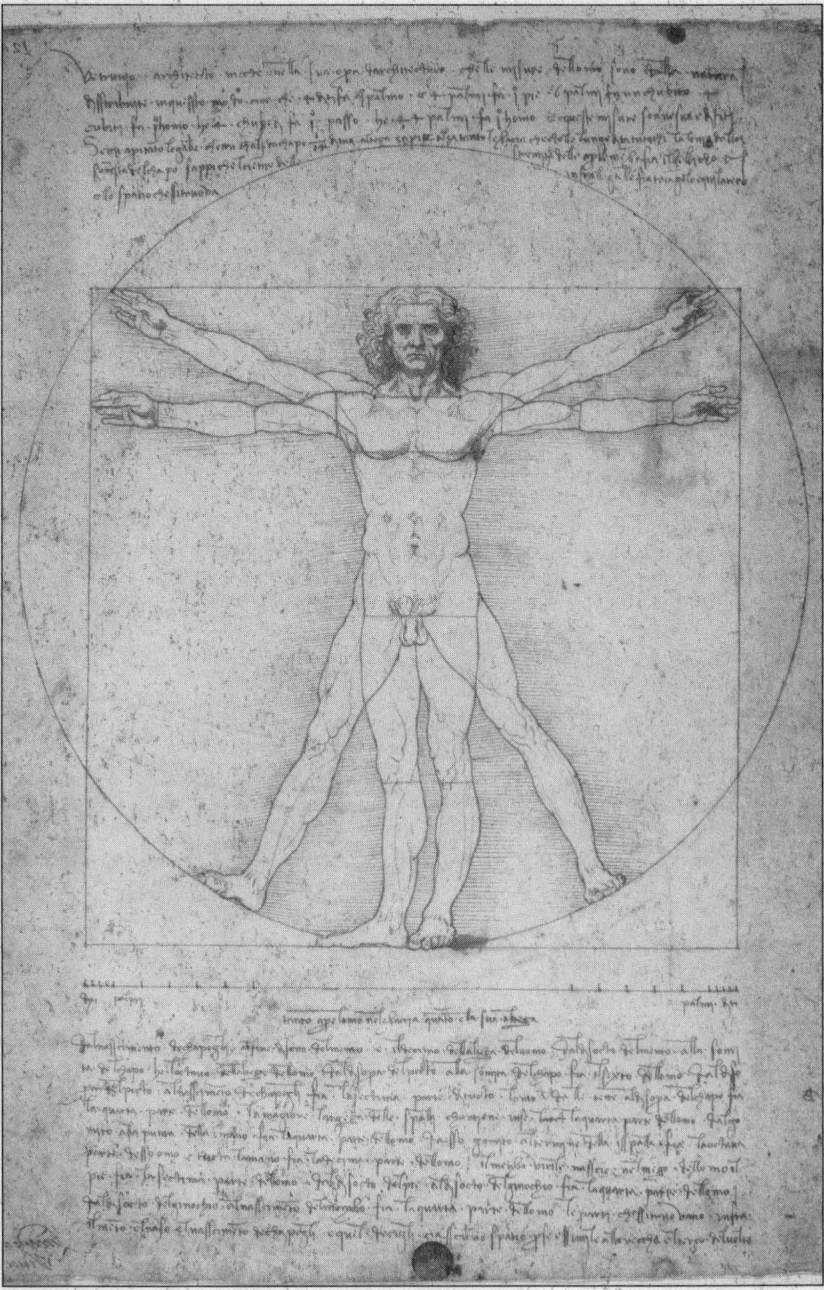

CHAPTER 10

Nurture Integration (Corporalità)

> As is the microcosm, so is the macrocosm.
> As is the atom, so is the universe.
> As is the human body, so is the cosmic body.
> As is the human mind, so is the cosmic mind.
>
> —HINDU SCRIPTURE

From Leonardo's notes on this drawing: "Vitruvius says in his work on architecture that the measurements of the human body are distributed by Nature as follows: four fingers make one palm; four palms make one foot; six palms make one cubit; four cubits make a man's height; and four cubits make one pace; and twenty-four palms make a man; and these measures he used in buildings."

Leonardo's *Vitruvian Man* was originally an illustration for a book entitled *De divinia proportione* (The divine proportion) by the Franciscan friar and mathematical innovator Luca Pacioli (1445–1517). Around 1496, over a decade after Leonardo went to Milan to serve as painter and engineer in the court of the duke of Milan, Pacioli arrived there to teach mathematics. Leonardo, who was passionately interested in mathematics, may have helped arrange his appointment to court, for the two men seemed to have been remarkably similar in sensibility, if Pacioli's book is any indication.

Pacioli opens his discussion of the "divine proportion," or "golden ratio," with a commentary on the proportions of the human body, observing that in mankind, "every sort of proportion and proportionality can be found, produced at the behest of God through the inner mysteries of nature." Remarks such as these make it clear why Leonardo would have found in Pacioli a mind and spirit *in simpatia* with his own. For both men the harmonious proportions of the human body were but one of the many "inner mysteries of nature" that served as a reflection of the perfection of their Creator.

While Pacioli's book may be little remembered, the famous illustration Leonardo did for it has never been forgotten. Just as the *Mona Lisa* has become a universal icon representing the balance of masculine and feminine energies, so Leonardo's *Vitruvian Man* has become a universal symbol of human potential and the integration of spirit, mind, and body. The image graces the jackets of books on personal development, the literature for health clubs and spas, the covers of brochures for medical centers and hospitals, and innumerable advertisements for products relating to health, fitness, and wellness.

Vitruvian Man takes its name from Roman architect Marcus Vitruvius (ca. 70–25 B.C.), who was the source of many of Pacioli's ideas. Vitruvius, sometimes known as "the first architect," analyzed the proportions of the human body from an architectural perspective:

> In the human body the central point is naturally the navel. For
> if a man be placed flat on his back, with his hands and feet ex-
> tended, and a pair of compasses centered at this navel, the fin-
> gers and toes of his two hands and feet will touch the
> circumference of a circle described therefrom. And just as the
> human body yields a circular outline, so too a square figure
> may be found from it. For if we measure the distance from the

soles of the feet to the top of the head, and then apply that measure to the outstretched arms, the breadth will be found to be the same as the height, as in the case of plane surfaces which are perfectly square.

Leonardo's appreciation for the concept of divine proportion was reflected in his drawings and paintings of people as well as in his architectural and city planning studies. But the Maestro's interest in the anatomy of the human body went far beyond a consideration of the proportions of its limbs or its usefulness as a blueprint for design. Through his pioneering anatomical investigations he sought to understand the body's innermost secrets, to enter into the very heart of creation, and in the process he came to a new understanding of health and healing—one that is remarkably prophetic of the holistic approach of many practitioners today. "Medicine is the restoration of discordant elements . . . infused into the living body," he wrote, and he believed that a harmonious integration of the elements of body and soul was essential to maintaining good health.

In his anatomical studies, as in everything else he did, Leonardo was always striving for the most all-encompassing type of understanding as well as the most detailed. He prefaces his notes on anatomy by promising: "I will speak of the functions of each part in every direction, putting before your eyes a description of the whole form and substance of man." He then describes his anatomical works as a *cosmografica del minor mondo*, a cosmography of the microcosm.

"Man was called the microcosmos by the ancients," he wrote, "and surely the term was well chosen." The notion of humankind as a microcosm of the greater world beyond is one of those central insights shared by all the great spiritual traditions: as above, so below.

The universality of this truth makes it as relevant today as it was for the ancients and for Leonardo. Moreover, the idea and its implications for health and healing are finding a new currency among contemporary practitioners of complementary medicine. Dr. Dale Schusterman, one of the most effective and powerful of this new breed of healers, states the core of the philosophy behind his work in language remarkably similar to Leonardo's: "The human body, and the energetic system that surrounds it, is a miniature replica of a larger, universal system."

Schusterman, a chiropractic physician, understands that true health is not just a matter of creating good alignment of the body but of aligning the physical with more subtle energies. Thus he wedded his initial training in spinal adjustment and kinesiology with a study of the world's great wisdom traditions, including the Jewish mysticism of the Kabbalah. He explains:

> The Kabbalah is based on the realization that man/woman is created in the image of a greater Cosmic or Divine Being. We should therefore be able, as Leonardo did, to see the cosmic design in our human form. In addition to our form's reflecting the higher pattern, our innate qualities of being are the same as those of the divine, as one drop of water has the properties of the ocean.

He adds:

> Kabbalistic images often relate to the human body. This is more than the anthropomorphizing of spiritual concepts; it is the relating of analogous structures between God and human.

Or, as Leonardo expressed it: "Our body is subject to heaven." Ajit Mookerjee, author of *Kundalini: The Arousal of the Inner Energy*, echoes Leonardo and Schusterman from a Hindu perspective:

> The forces governing the cosmos on the macro-level govern the individual on the micro-level. Life is one, and all its forms are interrelated in a vastly complicated but inseparable whole. The underlying unity becomes a bridge between the microcosm and the macrocosm.

Our Body Is Subject to Heaven

∞

"Know ye not that ye are the temple of God, and that
the Spirit of God dwelleth in you?"
—*1 Corinthians 3:16*

"Here . . . in this body of yours you do not perceive
the True, but there in fact it is. In that which is the
subtle essence, all that exists has its self. That is the
true, that is the Self, and thou . . . are That."
—*Chandogya Upanishad*

"The body is like clothing for the soul."
—*Gemara Shabbat*

"Christ has no body now on earth but yours,
no hands but yours, no feet but yours,
Yours are the eyes through which he is to look out
Christ's compassion to the world;
Yours are the feet with which he is to
go about doing good;
Yours are the hands with which he
is to bless men now."
—*St. Teresa of Ávila*

"I am the universal fire within the
body of living beings."
—Bhagavad Gita

∞

Leonardo's understanding of the relationship between micrososm and macrocosm, body and cosmos, began with his knowledge of the integration of body and mind. He knew that our attitudes and physiology were interdependent and that their integration must be consciously nurtured. Many have suggested that Leonardo's uncanny insight into the human body was a reflection of the way he himself lived, inner and outer being in harmony, resulting in physical grace and athletic achievements that were much admired in his time. In our own time Deepak Chopra describes him as "the seemingly perfect integration of mind, body, spirit and soul."

Anticipating the modern discipline of psychoneuroimmunology, which recognizes that our thinking is reflected in the strength of our immune response, Leonardo counseled, "He who would keep in good health" should remember to "avoid grievous moods and keep your mind cheerful." Leonardo himself was known to be even-tempered and optimistic, even when life was hard. He was also meticulous in his daily habits of eating, exercising, and resting. "Learn to preserve your own health," he advised. Though genetics and environment determine the cards that nature deals us, how we play those cards is up to us, with diet, exercise, and attitude key to achieving health and well-being, as Leonardo presciently understood.

Leonardo was highly critical of the practice of medicine in his day because much of it was based on superstition and clearly did more harm than good. He warned against the drugs doctors were prescribing, which he decried as products of unscientific "alchemy." While he would certainly have admired many of the drugs today's scientists have developed, as well as other advances that have been brought to us by modern medicine, he would have been aware of the shortcomings, particularly modern medicine's tendency to view patients as collections of individual parts rather than as interrelated wholes.

Although this way of thinking has begun to be challenged by forward-thinking practitioners, the reigning paradigm of medicine continues to be mechanistic. Physicians treat the body as a machine, each of whose parts is the purview of one or another specialist. And not only are the body's parts considered independent of one another, but the body itself is viewed as being independent of mind, emotion, spirit, and the surrounding environment. In an attempt to be objective, medical science turned us into objects. A specialist may know all about your ears, nose, or throat and a great deal about the rest of your body but hardly anything about your life or your overall condition or even the findings of another specialist whom you may have consulted about an apparently unrelated problem.

One problem with the failure to see the body as a whole, to engage in what is known as "systems thinking," is that modern Western medicine tends to focus on alleviating symptoms rather than addressing their underlying causes. New, more powerful drugs are constantly being developed in an attempt to suppress the manifestations of disease, and they often succeed. But they also create increasingly resistant viral and bacterial strains, as well as a wide range of side effects that can sometimes be worse than the original malady.

Leonardo believed in a much more holistic view of health. He wrote: "It is necessary for doctors who are the guardians of the sick to understand what man is, what life is, and what health is, and in what way a balance and harmony of these elements maintains it." This is the kind of insight that tends to get forgotten in our age of specialization, but Leonardo took a holistic, integrative approach to everything he studied in the natural world, plant, animal, or human, always seeking to make connections and to understand the relationship of the parts to the whole.

Traditional healing systems are much more likely than Western allopathic medicine to honor the wisdom of Leonardo's approach, which is why some of the practitioners of integrative medicine are now studying them for a deeper understanding of the origins of sickness and health. Dr. Rudolph Ballentine is a leader in the movement to analyze the relative strengths and weaknesses of the world's diverse healing traditions, comparing conventional Western medicine to Indian Ayurveda, traditional Chinese medicine, homeopathy, European and Native American herbology, nutrition, and psychotherapeutic bodywork. Ballentine seeks to bring together the best practices of these diverse traditions. "By integrating them, superimposing one upon another in layer after layer of complementary perspectives and techniques," he writes, "we can arrive at an amalgam that is far more potent and thorough than any one of them taken alone."

The aptly named Mona Lisa Schulz, M.D., Ph.D., is another of the leading figures in the contemporary renaissance of Leonardo-like thinking as it applies to healing. A neuropsychiatrist, scientist, medical intuitive, and author of *Awakening Intuition,* Schulz echoes Leonardo's advice that we must "learn to preserve our own health," and shares his belief that good health requires that we "avoid grievous moods and keep the mind cheerful." "If your emotions are imbalanced," she writes, "there will be a proportional degree of biochemical imbalance in your body that will set the scene for illness. Similarly, if your physical health is neglected, your mood would be disrupted in an equivalent fashion."

Marco De Vries, M.D., Ph.D., is the author of *The Redemption of the Intangible in Medicine* and a leader in the integration of spiritual and scientific approaches to healing. In 1980 De Vries conducted a pioneering experiment into the power of meaning in his patients' lives.

Working with patients who had been referred to him by their general practitioners because they had not responded well to treatment, Dr. De Vries asked them to participate in discussion groups. In six half-hour sessions the patients, who were suffering from a wide range of ailments, discussed among themselves and with the De Vries research team such basic questions as:

- ✦ What do you really want to live for?
- ✦ What do you need to do to be well?
- ✦ How could you do what you need to do to be well?

+ What does your innate wisdom tell you about your
  condition?

De Vries describes the goal of this experiment as helping patients to "consider their physical condition and situation from
the perspective of meaning in life." The result?

All patients progressed by changing their attitudes towards
themselves and towards their physical complaints. In addition,
at the end of the six sessions all patients experienced a change
in their physical complaints; overall, the physical complaints
became less dominant, and in some cases the physical complaints disappeared. One patient, in particular, dramatically
changed the course of her medical history: at the age of
twenty-eight she stopped taking tranquilizers which she had
been using continually for fourteen years in high doses. In so
choosing and acting on her choice, she experienced a sense of
identity and meaning for the first time in many years.

Leonardo's vision of wholeness is alive in the emerging paradigm of integrative medicine. His systems orientation guides us to
create a new kind of medicine based on a harmonious integration
of the best of the world's healing traditions and the most valuable
data from all the sciences, including genetics, chemistry, physics,
and psychology. Above all, his integrative approach can inspire us
to remember the role of the human spirit in health and healing.

The word *healing* comes from the root *hal,* which means
"making whole." Leonardo sought to understand nothing less
than the "whole form and substance of man" and to use that understanding to develop knowledge of "what life is, and what
health is." Remember that the paradigm of healing you hold
may be a powerful determinant of your quality of life. If you
nurture an awareness of the unity of body, emotion, mind, and
spirit, you'll discover a deeper sense of wholeness—of divine
proportion.

Nurture Integration: Self-Assessment

ℭℴ

☐ I view my body as a mechanical object.

☐ I view my body as a system of energy.

☐ I take responsibility for my health and well-being.

☐ I'm aware of the ways in which my attitude affects my bodily state.

☐ I'm aware of the ways in which my bodily state affects my attitude.

☐ I am sensitive to the flow of energy through my body.

☐ I experience a harmony between the flow of energy in my body and the flow of energy in the world around me.

☐ I experience my body as a temple of the spirit.

☐ I experience the quality of the sacred in my enjoyment of sex.

⚘ Nurture Integration: Spiritual Practices

LEONARDO'S *VITRUVIAN MAN* HEALING EXERCISE

Leonardo's *Vitruvian Man,* his representation of the "cosmography of the microcosm," is the inspiration behind a healing practice developed by Dr. Dale Schusterman. I discovered this, much to my delight, when I asked him to contribute a practice for this chapter, and it turned out—not too surprisingly, given his philosophy—that the *Vitruvian Man* image was the basis of an exercise he uses to teach patients how to integrate mind, body, and spirit. This exercise is a perfect embodiment of Leonardo's ideal of harmony and balance.

The practice described below applies knowledge of the "anatomy" of the universal system, or macrocosm, to the human system, or microcosm. Based on teachings from the Kabbalah, Hindu cosmology, and yogic science, it brings the body and mind into alignment with the higher realm. The result is an enhanced experience of wholeness and integration.

Schusterman explains: "One reason the *Vitruvian Man* serves as a global icon of holistic healing and symbol of wholeness is that this composite image evokes the energy of the four dimensions of reality. Looking at this drawing causes an integrative energy shift in all who view it."

Leonardo's four-in-one drawing depicts two different arm postures and two different leg postures. Each arm position can be

combined with each leg position, resulting in a total of four different possible stances. According to Schusterman, these four body
postures reflect the energy states of the four levels of mankind—
"physical, astral, causal, and spiritual. Although different systems
of thought have different labels for them," he says, "the idea of the
four dimensions is almost universal. They are often called 'bodies,'
as they are imaged as shells of energy that surround the physical
body, with each one becoming less dense as it moves away from
the physical. From the astral level we obtain our psychic senses and
we often visit this world in our dreams. The causal body is experienced in deep sleep and is the realm where we tap into what Jung
called the 'collective unconscious.' This is the realm of connection
to archetypes. The highest world is the spiritual world where the 'I
am' or ultimate witness state of an individual exists. What we call
God is beyond the four bodies and defies description."

The four realms are described in more detail in Schusterman's
informative and very useful book *Sign Language of the Soul*. But
Schusterman agrees that it isn't necessary to understand or embrace
the four-realm model in order to get full benefit from this practice.

As explained step by step below, you can begin using the
Vitruvian Man image for healing and integration by assuming
each of the individual postures yourself. Like yoga *asanas,* they
serve to tune the body to a more harmonious energy frequency.
In other words, when you assume these postures, a deep part of
you recognizes a connection with a higher vibration of consciousness, and your nervous system attunes to this new level.
Doing the steps in sequence should restore harmony. As you repeat the sequence seven times, as is recommended, you will access not just physical but spiritual harmony.

This exercise may be done standing or lying on your back.
Refer to the image at the beginning of this chapter for the arm
and leg positions, remembering to turn the left foot outward and
have the palms facing forward in each of the four postures. You'll
get the most from this procedure if you maintain a quiet, receptive witnessing state throughout. In other words, simply observe

yourself observing yourself doing the postures. Hold each posture for three to five seconds and then proceed to the next one.

1. Start with the legs apart, left foot turned outward, and the arms in the horizontal position.

2. Keep the arms in the horizontal position and bring the legs together (remember to keep the left foot turned outward in all five steps).

3. Keep the legs together and raise the arms to the upper position.

4. Keep the arms in the upper position and separate the legs.

Once you do these four simple steps, your body will be centered, although some imbalance may remain in your system. Take a moment to experience your new centered state, then move to the next step of the exercise, a very simple one.

5. Look at the composite picture of the *Vitruvian Man* at the beginning of this chapter. This should resolve any residual imbalance, moving you toward a more complete integration of your body, energy, and spirit. Repeat these five steps seven times.

Some people experience a profound sense of relief from this, while others just notice a very subtle feeling of inner harmony. I find this practice to be a wonderful tune-up—it always makes me feel better. After learning this exercise, Taya-Marie Levine, an organizational consultant and executive coach from Virginia, wrote the following note to Dr. Schusterman, which is representative of the kind of response this practice evokes: "The *Vitruvian Man* balancing method lets me, within seconds, address any physical or other inner disturbance I may be aware of. There is no denying that the composite image at the end of the sequence brings immediate and evident shifts at an energetic level. I can use it wherever I am, in my office, at home, or when traveling, because all the resource I need is my knowledge of how to do it. In this case, I am the resource, and I couldn't be more grateful for that!"

You'll get the most benefit if you practice this exercise every morning and evening. It is particularly valuable to do when you are feeling tired or stressed.

An alternative way to do this procedure if you are at work, or if for some reason you are unable to make one or more of the postures, is to look at images of the individual postures in sequence and then look at the whole image. If you go to the following website, you will find a slide show of the five images, which you can look at over and over: www.SignLanguageoftheSoul.com/leonardo.html.

LEONARDO'S COMMENTARY ON THE *VITRUVIAN MAN*

"If you open your legs so much as to decrease your height by 1/14 and spread and raise your arms so that your middle fingers are on a level with the top of your head, you must know that the navel will be the centre of a circle of which the outspread limbs touch the circumference; and the space between the legs will form an equilateral triangle. The span of a man's outspread arms is equal to his height.

"The painter in his harmonious proportions makes the component parts react simultaneously so that they can be seen at one and the same time both together and separately; together, by viewing the design of the composition as a whole; and separately by viewing the design of its component parts."

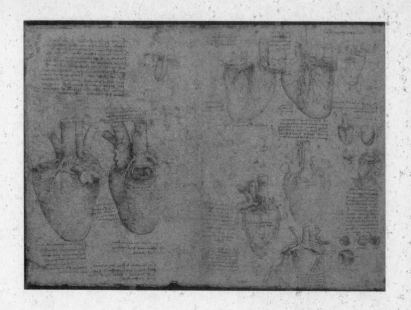

HEALING FROM THE ENERGY OF THE HEART
EXERCISE: *AHAVAH/ANANDA*

In Hebrew, the word for "love" is *ahavah*. In Sanskrit, the word for "bliss"—which is closer to spiritual love than our normal conception of human love—is *ananda*. Because Hebrew and Sanskrit are ancient languages that are less divorced from their spiritual roots than the languages we use today, the sound of these ancient words evokes the energetic significance of their meaning. So simply saying them aloud will bring you into the presence of what they stand for. Similarly, Leonardo's drawing of the human heart emits the energetic frequency of spiritual love.

Try the following: look at Leonardo's image of the heart and then say aloud the word *ahavah* or *ananda*. The resulting resonance between what you see in the picture and what you hear in the word will be powerful. Those who are sensitive to subtle energy will feel this immediately.

The energy of the heart holds a powerful secret to healing on many levels. Emmet Fox, author and inspiration to Alcoholics

Anonymous founder Bill Wilson, commented on the healing power of *ahavah:*

> There is no difficulty that enough love will not conquer; no disease that enough love will not heal; no door that enough love will not open; no gulf that enough love will not bridge; no wall that enough love will not throw down; no sin that enough love will not redeem. . . .
>
> It makes no difference how deeply seated may be the trouble; how hopeless the outlook; how muddled the tangle; how great the mistake. A sufficient realization of love will dissolve it all. If only you could love enough you would be the happiest and most powerful being in the world.

THE HEART'S ENERGY

It might interest you to know that the heart's electromagnetic field is the most powerful the body produces. According to Doc Childre, the author of *The HeartMath Solution,* "It's approximately five thousand times greater in strength than the field produced by the brain. The heart's field not only permeates every cell in the body but also radiates outside of us; it can be measured up to eight to ten feet away with sensitive detectors called magnetometers."

Modern research confirms that ambidexterity promotes balance and brain development. Not surprisingly, Leonardo was ambidextrous. But most of us rely on one highly dominant hand and side. The side we do not use may then become the repository for the energetic detritus of the many parts of ourselves that we would rather not face. In other words, when we move away from inner truth, or close off our hearts, we store the memory of this in neglected areas of our nervous system. Thus, writing, drawing, or otherwise engaging the nondominant hand can help us toward energetic as well as psychophysical balance.

We can use this principle of ambidexterity in conjunction with Leonardo's image of the heart to access and begin to clear deep imbalances within our bodies and minds. The following simple exercise will help bring imbalances in your system to the surface so that you can clear them. Before you begin, please do the *Vitruvian Man* healing exercise a few times. This will prepare you to metabolize the imbalances that may arise through this practice.

Get an unlined blank piece of paper and a pen or pencil. Write your name on the paper using your nondominant hand, without looking at what you are writing. If you are right-handed, then use your left hand, and vice versa.

Write your name again using the nondominant hand, this time while looking at Leonardo's drawing of the heart on page 147. Look at the picture of the heart, not at what you are writing. Since this picture carries the frequency of *ahavah* (love) and *ananda* (bliss), you will be bringing this energy to the nondominant, hidden side of yourself. All you need to do is write your name while looking at the heart image.

After writing your name with your nondominant hand while looking at Leonardo's drawing of the heart, sit quietly for a moment to sense internal changes. This simple exercise may bring up unfamiliar feelings or unusual movements of energy in your body, although not everyone is sensitive to these feelings.

Now do one final repetition of the *Vitruvian Man* healing exercise, to ensure that you are balanced.

VITRUVIAN CENTERING EXERCISE

Leonardo's famous canon-of-proportion figure shows that the arms and legs are equidistant from the body's center of gravity. This center of gravity is called the *hara* in Japan and the lower *tan-tien* in China. In the West we call it guts. You can improve your balance and nurture integration of body, mind, and spirit by cultivating an awareness of your center. Begin by sitting or standing upright; then, with either hand, press the point on your belly two finger widths down from your navel. Inhale gently through your nose and direct your breath down to your center. Exhale slowly through your mouth with a gentle, continuous "ahhhh," maintaining an awareness of your center as you exhale. Do this seven times with full awareness to center yourself, and then remember to breathe into your center from time to time throughout the course of your day.

QI GONG ELEMENTS PRACTICE

Dean Deng, M.D., is one of the most centered, energetic people I've ever met. He is also a unique paragon of integrative medicine. In addition to his training as a medical doctor, Deng was initiated into the ancient lineage of Taoist qi gong at age three and is a master of this remarkable system. Qi gong practice forms the basis of all the healing and martial arts of China. *Qi*, pronounced "chee," is the vital force in nature, and *gong* can be translated as "work, practice and become powerful." So, qi gong is a way of working that strengthens the power of your vital force.

A growing body of scientific research demonstrates that qi gong practice can promote coherence of the brain waves between the two sides of the cerebral cortex, increase white blood cell count, and improve circulation and endocrine production, among many other benefits.

Dr. Deng has found qi gong practice particularly helpful in the following areas:

+ Stress management
+ Strengthening nervous and immune systems
+ Purifying and rejuvenating the whole body, including internal organs, bones, circulation, skin, and muscles
+ Reducing or eliminating pain
+ Promoting a sense of well-being
+ Healing a wide range of specific ailments

I was very lucky to have the opportunity to work with Dr. Deng on a regular basis for a few years and to attend his training workshop, "Eight Treasures of Qi Gong." The Eight Treasures is a fifteen-minute practice that offers many of the benefits described above. You can learn it through Dr. Deng's book and video *Qi Gong: A Legacy of Chinese Healing*. In the meantime, you can try this Leonardian adaptation of one of Dr. Deng's warm-up exercises to give you a taste of this integrating, vivifying practice.

Leonardo attempted to draw the essence of the elements of earth, fire, water, and air. In this simple six-part exercise, you will draw on the essence of those same elements to energize all the cells of your body.

Stand upright, feet shoulder width apart, shoulders relaxed, knees slightly bent. Enjoy a few cycles of breath into the base of your belly, the lower *tan-tien*. As you breathe, imagine that you are inhaling subtle *qi*, the life force.

1. **Drawing the energy of the earth.** Keeping your feet firmly on the floor, hold your arms straight out in front of you at chest height, palms facing down. Exhale as you sink straight down by bending your knees, and inhale as you straighten up again. As you sink and rise rhythmically, imagine that you are drawing the energy of the earth through the soles of your feet. Feel the energy that grows a garden and sustains a forest or a field of golden wheat flowing up from the earth to fill every cell of your body. Do eight repetitions.

2. **Drawing the energy of the sun.** Exhale as you reach your hands straight out from your chest, palms opening out as though you were reaching for the sun. Inhale as you draw your hands back toward your chest, imagining that you are filling your body with the healing golden light. Do eight repetitions.

3. **Drawing the energy of the ocean.** Bring your palms together in front of your chest, exhale as you open your arms out to the sides as wide as you can (like the *Vitruvian Man* image), inhale, and bring your hands back to the center of your chest as you imagine washing all the molecules of your body with the wonderful energy of the ocean. Repeat for eight full cycles.

4. **Drawing the energy of the sky.** Raise both arms straight up over your head as you inhale. Bring your arms around and down in a big circle as you exhale. Raise your arms straight up again and imagine filling your circle with the energy of the sky, stars, and new moon. Repeat eight times.

5. **Drawing the energy of the whole universe.** Raise your arms straight up as you inhale and bring them straight down as you exhale and imagine concentrating all the energy of the earth, sun, ocean, and sky—the whole universe—into your center.

6. **Belly laughing.** Dr. Deng has one of the most vibrant smiles I've ever seen and one of the most resonant laughs I've

ever heard. He told me that his big belly laugh is the real secret of his amazing *qi* power. So please complete this practice by patting your belly as vigorously as you can and repeating the mantra "Ha ha ha ha." If you have trouble belly laughing, please try this remedial Zen meditation until you achieve enlaughenment: Sit in an upright position. Close your eyes and repeat this mantra very slowly three times: "Zen-za-hu-ma." Repeat three more times a little faster, then again as quickly as you can.

SPIRITUAL DECISIONS

Dr. John Diamond, M.D., author of *Life Energy: Unlocking the Hidden Power of Your Emotions to Achieve Total Well-Being*, expresses the influence of our power of choice and its effect on health from a spiritual perspective:

The course through life
is determined
by hundreds of thousands,
millions of choices.
What to feel, what to want,
What to say, what to eat, what to do.
And each and every choice
is for health, for love and for God
—or not.
Thus all are spiritual decisions.

ractice Love (Connessione)

Sane and insane, all are searching lovelorn
For Him, in mosque, temple, church, alike.
For only God is the One God of Love, And Love
calls from all these, each one His home.

—SUFI WISDOM

From his early paintings *Annunciation* and *Adoration of the Magi* through his two versions of *Madonna of the Rocks*, his *Madonna of the Yarnwinder, Madonna and Child with Cats, Benois Madonna,* and his two versions of *Virgin and Child with St. Anne,* Leonardo never stopped seeking to portray the face of divine love. The adoring face of the Virgin is our symbol for the seventh principle, *connessione*: practice love.

"The idea of love," according to a global survey of the world's spiritual traditions reported in the *Encyclopedia of*

This is a close-up of the face of the Virgin Mary from one of Leonardo's two versions of *Virgin and Child with St. Anne.* The Maestro's representation of the face of divine love served as a powerful inspiration for Raphael and many other great masters.

Love: "The Single Most Potent Force"

"God is love, and he who abides in love abides in
God, and God abides in him."
—*Christianity, 1 John 4:16*

"It makes no difference as to the name of God, since
love is the real God of all the world."
—*Native American wisdom*

"The glorious one God of love."
—*Hinduism, Upanishads*

"Love has no cause;
it is the astrolabe of God's secrets."
—*Sufism, Rumi*

"The world is built of love."
—*Judaism, King David*

"Love and compassion are necessities, not luxuries.
Without them, humanity cannot survive."
—*Tibetan Buddhism, Dalai Lama*

Religion, "has left a wider and more indelible imprint upon the development of human culture in all its aspects than any other single notion." The *Encyclopedia* reports that leaders from diverse traditions all seem to agree "that love is the single most potent force in the universe, a cosmic impulse that creates, maintains, directs, informs . . . every living thing."

Amor vincit omnia, the ancient Latin phrase meaning "love conquers all," was one of Leonardo's mottoes, expressing his own awareness of love as the "most potent force in the universe."

✥ Loving Through Being

For Leonardo, love was the force through which everything was connected to everything else, and his never-ending *curiosità* was the channel that led him to love. "The love of anything," he wrote, "is the fruit of our knowledge of it, and grows as our knowledge deepens." Love was at the very core of his consciousness. As he expressed it: "Love alone makes me remember, it is only love that makes me aware."

Leonardo's art portrays plants and animals as well as people with uncanny structural and anatomical accuracy—an accuracy born of the closest observation. What we sense in these intimate depictions of nature is Leonardo's love for God's works, his passion to reveal "the glories of natural design" through his art. Vision—the eye, in which "the beauty of the world is mirrored"—was his route to capturing the very soul of nature, and painting what his eye saw was his way of practicing his love of the Divine. The more Leonardo devoted himself to learning about the world, the more readily he saw the connections between past and present and among all forms of nature—human and animal, animate and inanimate.

One stunning example of Leonardo's attempt to depict the unity of creation through his art is his unfinished painting *Adoration of the Magi,* which was commissioned by the monks of San Donato at Scopeto for the altarpiece of their church. In this painting the complexity of the composition, the innovative use of perspective, and the contrasting lights and darks serve almost as magnets to focus the energy of all the figures depicted in the painting on the central drama—the Virgin and Child receiving the magi. As the magi pay tribute in the foreground, scenes of ruin and devastation in the background signal the fall of the pagan world, which was set in motion by the birth of Christ. Leonardo seems to have in mind nothing less than a summation

of all human history in this painting, with the arrival of Christ as the climactic moment. Thus the Virgin and Child are depicted as the still center of a whirlwind of emotion that radiates beyond them, building to ever greater heights and intensity the farther from the center the figures appear.

The tension between the tranquillity of the Divine and the turbulence of human experience prefigures the Maestro's more evolved expression of this contrast in *The Last Supper*. But in *The Last Supper*, the figures of the disciples at the table with Christ are clear and distinct; in this painting Leonardo arranges the figures at odd angles in space so that they fade away as though into infinity, an effect that suggests that they are innumerable and thus representative of all humanity. In the background, the architectural ruins and equestrian battle scenes convey the bankruptcy, confusion, and chaos of a world without the message of love, which is being brought by the unfinished but majestic figure of the Christ child in his mother's arms. Many critics have commented on the prominence of the carob tree, which is not only the tree from which Judas hanged himself but also the tree whose pods sustained St. John in the wilderness. Behind the carob tree is a palm tree, a symbol of life with its fanlike leaves radiating out from the trunk, just as the arteries and veins proceed from the heart—or, as Leonardo expressed it, "The heart is the nut which produces the tree of the veins."

On the far left and right of the painting we see the introduction of another favorite Leonardo theme: the contrast of youth and beauty (represented by the elegant young man on the far right) with age and wisdom (represented by the ancient man on the immediate left of the Virgin). But for Leonardo, opposites are never simply opposites. As with pleasure and pain, youth and age are twinned, the one contained within the other. The youthful figure—which many have surmised was a self-portrait—will one day be the old man, and if the young man makes that connection, he has within him the seeds of a good old age. "Knowledge acquired in one's youth arrests the damage of old age," Leonardo wrote, "and if you understand that old age has wisdom for its sustenance, you will so conduct yourself in youth that your old age will not lack nourishment."

THE GENETIC CODE OF THE UNIVERSE

The "true eye" will see recurring motifs—artistic as well as scientific—throughout Leonardo's body of work. He was fascinated by the ripples flowing from a stone thrown into water, the vortices of whirlpools and tornadoes. His paintings and drawings show his endless preoccupation with the patterns made by the cascading of hair, the draping of garments, and the swirling tendrils of plants. And the spiraling and double-spiraling motifs that

LIKE LOVE, WATER FLOWS THROUGH EVERYTHING

For Leonardo, water was one of the elements that bind all together. In words that recall his tree trunk/heart analogy, he wrote in his observations on the nature of water: "As from the pool of blood proceed the veins which spread their branches through the human body, in just the same manner the ocean fills the body of the earth with an infinite number of veins of water." But his poetic vision of rivers and streams as the arteries and veins of a living being was more than just a metaphor. His discovery that death in old men is often caused by a clogging of the arteries was undoubtedly influenced by his observation of the way silt collects at the mouth of rivers, damming their flow.

The vivifying presence of water throughout Leonardo's art is beautifully expressed in this passage from Walter Pater: "You may follow it springing from its distant source among the rocks on the heath . . . as a goodly river . . . below the cliffs of the *Madonna of the Rocks*, washing the white walls of its distant villages, stealing out in a network of divided streams in *La Gioconda* to the seashore of the *Saint Anne*— that delicate place, where the wind passes like the hand of some fine etcher over the surface, and the untorn shells are lying thick upon the sand, and the tops of the rocks, to which the waves never rise, are green with grass, grown fine as hair. It is the landscape, not of dreams or of fancy, but of places far withdrawn, and hours selected from a thousand with a miracle of finesse. Through Leonardo's strange veil of sight things reached him so; in no ordinary night or day, but as in faint light of an eclipse, or in some brief interval of falling rain at daybreak, or through deep water."

we see in so many of his paintings—the pose and clothing of his St. John, the intertwining of Leda and the swan, the twisting figure of his St. Jerome—are echoed in his inventions: the volute gear, the olive press, the variety of screws, the double staircase. His interest in all these helical forms suggests that he had intuited the essential unity of all living things, as though he anticipated the twentieth-century discovery of the double helix, the very foundation of life.

Although it is based on observation and scientific analysis, not on any religious philosophy, Leonardo's intuiting of the pattern that links everything together, making all creation one, is also reflected in universal spiritual wisdom.

Physicist David Bohm refers to this universal pattern as the "implicate order," a "deep structure" of connectedness binding all the elements of the world. In 1980 Bohm wrote, "Everything is enfolded into everything." Five centuries earlier Leonardo noted, "Everything comes from everything, and everything is made out of everything, and everything returns to everything."

Bohm's theory of the holographic universe posits that the macrocosm and microcosm are indeed one—that the "genetic code" of the universe is held in every atom just as a strand of DNA holds the entire genetic code of an individual. Leonardo seems to have reached a similar conclusion: "This is the real miracle, that all shapes, all colors, all images of every part of the universe are concentrated in a single point."

And just as everything is connected to everything, it emerges from and returns to nothing. In the words of Leonardo:

> Nothingness has no center, and its boundaries are nothingness. . . . Among the great things which are found among us the existence of Nothing is the greatest . . . its essence dwells as regards time between the past and the future, and possesses nothing of the present. . . . This Nothingness has the part equal to the whole and the whole to the part, the divisible to the indivisible, and it comes to the same amount whether we divide it or multiply it or add to it or subtract from it."

"This vastness is not empty or a void or impersonal
but filled with the incandescent nectar of
selfless love, tender joy, and gratitude."
—*Prajnaparamita Sutra*

The Maestro describes the longing to return to the ultimate source of being as an expression of our inseparability from nature:

> Every part is disposed to unite with the whole, that it may thereby escape from its own incompleteness.

And he adds,

> This longing is in its quintessence the spirit of the elements, which . . . desires continually to return to its source. And I would have you know that this same longing is in its quintessence inherent in nature.

Once again his words are hauntingly similar to the universal wisdom expressed by Lao-tzu in the *Tao-te Ching:*

> The movement of the Way is a return;
> In weakness lies its major usefulness.
> From What-is all the world of things was born
> But What-is sprang in turn from What-is-not.

Leonardo reminds us to face the mystery of the boundless, timeless nothingness from which we all emerge and to which we will all return—and to face it with a smile.

Perhaps he knew as he prepared to return to nothingness that as the Catholic monk Thomas Merton noted, "There is nothing so close to God as stillness." Except, perhaps, love.

Love: Oneness in Diversity

"One must know that no existing thing has an
independent existence. One must know that
all things are interdependent."
—Precepts of the Masters, *Tibetan Buddhist text*

"Deep down the consciousness of mankind is one."
—*David Bohm, physicist*

"It really boils down to this: that all life is interrelated.
We are all caught in an inescapable network of
mutuality, tied to a single garment of destiny.
Whatever affects one directly, affects all indirectly."
—*Rev. Martin Luther King Jr.*

"The world and I have a common origin and all
creatures and I together are one."
—*Chuang-tzu*

"Whenever we try to pick out anything by itself, we
find it hitched to everything else in the universe."
—*John Muir, naturalist*

"Behold but One in all things."
—*Kabir, Persian poet*

"All things, material and spiritual, originate from one
source and are related as if they were one family."
—*Morihei Ueshiba, founder of aikido*

"Hear, O Israel, the Lord our God is one Lord."
—*The essential prayer of Judaism*

Practice Love: Self-Assessment

❧

☐ I feel connected to something greater than my own ego.

☐ I consciously nurture my connection to something greater than myself every day.

☐ I practice conscious lovingkindness with my parents and other relatives.

☐ I practice conscious lovingkindness with my colleagues and associates at work.

☐ I practice conscious lovingkindness with the people I interact with on an incidental basis (waiters, salesclerks, tollbooth attendants, and other so-called strangers).

☐ I allow myself to experience the fullness of love, giving and receiving, in my life every day.

✢ Practice Love: Spiritual Practices

"From Love we are born
It is Love that sustains us
It is unto Love that we return."

—UPANISHADS

DO GOOD

In 1976 I returned to London after a three-week adventure in Turkey, where I experienced the powerful *zhikr* of the Halveti dervishes and was also especially blessed with the opportunity to receive an initiation from the remarkable Sufi master Hassan Shushud.

Then, shortly after my return, I received word that the renowned Sufi teacher Sheikh Nazim al-Haqqani, the Fortieth Link in the Golden Chain of the Naqshbandia, which leads back to the Prophet Muhammad, was coming from Damascus to lead prayers and share his teaching in London. I traveled across town for this wonderful opportunity with a sense of tremendous anticipation. The living room of the home where the sheik was to speak was packed, and the spiritual electricity known as *baraka* filled the air. The sheik entered the room wearing his elegant green robe and white turban. The silence was palpable as we waited for his words. And then he spoke: "Do good; don't do bad." He smiled and left the room. Although at the time it seemed a bit like a moment out of a *New Yorker* cartoon, this penetrating dose of the obvious is all too easy to forget in a postmodern culture that often worships narcissistic relativism and celebrity above charity and goodness.

While it is good to search our souls, sharpen our awareness, free ourselves from attachment, integrate the four dimensions of energy, balance masculine and feminine, and engage our shadows, it is most important of all to practice goodness. Kindness, forgiveness, charity, and service are the cornerstones of the Way in every tradition.

As Leonardo wrote: "Virtue is our true good and the true reward of its possessor." The Maestro offers the following poetic advice to cultivate the love of virtue: "It clings always to pure and virtuous things and takes up its abode in a noble heart; as the birds do in green woods on flowery branches." Once again, the Maestro's words are echoed in universal wisdom, this time in the words of Buddha: "Set your heart on doing good. Do it over and over again, and you will be filled with joy."

Here are a few simple practices to invite goodness and love into your life:

PRACTICE LEVEL SEVEN CHARITY

Every spiritual tradition promotes the ideal of charity. In the Christian tradition, charity is the greatest of virtues as it represents God's pure love. In Islam it is one of the five fundamentals. Called *zakat*, which translates as "purification," it is to be given purely to please Allah. For Buddhists, charity is one of the six requirements and is to be performed without consideration of personal loss or benefit.

But, like so many other wonderful things, charity is easily commingled with ego when, for example, it is given to gain personal recognition or influence. Then it becomes just another tool of self-aggrandizement.

The great Jewish physician and philosopher Moses Maimonides established a hierarchy of giving that offers a guide to practicing charity while remaining free from the pollution of egotism. According to Maimonides, there are seven levels of charity, listed below in ascending order of purity of intention:

1. The donor gives unwillingly.
2. The donor gives only after being asked for the donation.
3. The donor is asked for charity and gives it directly to the recipient with a smile. (The donor is clearly deriving pleasure from the act, and the recipient may feel ashamed.)
4. The donor and recipient are aware of each other, but the donation is made before the recipient asks for it.
5. The donor does not know the recipient, but the recipient does know who the donor is. (The recipient may feel beholden to the donor.)
6. The donor knows to whom he or she gives, but the recipient does not know the donor. (The benefactor may have some amount of pleasure and a sense of power over the recipient.)
7. Both donor and recipient are unaware of each other. Giving that is anonymous on both sides is performing a mitzvah (good act) for the sake of performing a mitzvah. The donor doesn't know who is being helped, so there is less of a sense of self-importance, and the recipient doesn't feel beholden to anyone specific.

Maimonides balances his emphasis on the purity of the giver's intention with the ultimate efficacy of the results the giving produces. He taught that the greatest charity strengthens the receiver so that there is no longer a need for charity.

PERFORM CONSCIOUS SERVICE

Nobel prize–winning author and Hindu sage Rabindranath Tagore shared his enlightenment regarding the mitzvah of service in these words: "I awoke and saw that life was service. I acted and behold, service was joy." And Gandhi observed, "All other pleasures and possessions pale into nothingness before service which is rendered in a spirit of joy."

In your notebook, make a list of seven simple acts of service that you could perform in the course of a week. Examples might include cooking a meal for a friend, cleaning a room for a relative, picking up the litter on the grounds of your office, babysitting for a young couple, or volunteering at a homeless shelter or hospital. Then do one each day for a week. Don't talk about it; just record your reflections in your notebook.

> "How many emperors, how many princes have there been of whom no memory remains, yet they strove only after territory and wealth to secure their reputations? How many have there been who lived in material poverty in order to enrich their lives with virtue? The poor man has been much more successful than the rich in this goal, as virtue surpasses wealth. Do you not see that the treasure in itself does not heap praise on its accumulator after his life is spent?"
>
> —*Leonardo da Vinci*

PRACTICE COMPASSION AND FORGIVENESS

Compassion is at the heart of all the world's great spiritual traditions. Please read the words below and reflect on how you can bring them to life in your heart, now.

From the Jewish tradition: "As we recall the compassion shown to us by our parents, so may we dedicate ourselves to turning that compassion toward all the inhabitants of the earth."

In the words of the Buddha: "Hate never yet dispelled hate. Only love dispels hate. That is the law, ancient and inexhaustible."

Through the lessons of Christ: "Malice will never drive out malice. But if someone does evil to you, you should do good to him, so that by your good work you may destroy his malice."

In the exhortation of the Prophet Muhammad: "Forgive those who wrong you; join those who cut you off; do good to those who do evil to you."

SPIRALING BREATH MEDITATION

We know that Leonardo loved spirals. We see them over and over again in his work—in the curling hair in the portrait of Ginevra de' Benci, the whorling tendrils of his favorite plant, the Star of Bethlehem, the helical structure of the nautilus shells he loved to collect. Just as they are part of the deep structure of connectedness that links all living things together, as is the water that ripples and streams across the earth, so too is the air we all breathe. As Leonardo noted, "Our vital powers are derived from the air which is the common living principle of the human race and of other living creatures." The following spiraling-breath meditation is a literally inspiring way to celebrate the spirit of the Maestro and open yourself to a deeper connection to yourself, to nature, and to the Divine.

Begin by sitting or standing comfortably, with your spine lengthened and your shoulders relaxed. Close your eyes. Imagine, as you inhale, that pure white light is spiraling up from the earth through the bottom of your feet in a counterclockwise rotation. As the breath and light spiral up through your spine and out through the top of your head, imagine them washing all the cells in their path, cleansing, purifying, and refreshing every part of you. As you exhale, imagine the breath and light flowing down from above, through the top of your head, and then down through your spine to your feet and back to the earth in a clockwise spiraling pattern. As the breath and light spiral down, allow all your cells to be filled with vitality and love. Do seven cycles of spiraling breath. Then open your eyes, breathe normally, and pause for a moment to give thanks. (You can learn a more detailed version of this meditation by consulting the wonderful book by my dear friend Wendy Palmer entitled *The Intuitive Body*.)

CONNESSIONE THROUGH CONSCIOUS LOVINGKINDNESS

You can cultivate your spiritual *connessione* through a simple meditation drawn from the Buddhist tradition. The practice is called *metta*, which translates as "lovingkindness."

It involves making four threefold requests or invocations. You begin by asking: "May I be happy. May I be peaceful. May I be free." (The Buddhist ideal of freedom involves liberating your soul from the wheel of death and rebirth so that you can return, voluntarily, as a bodhisattva to work for the enlightenment and liberation of all sentient beings. Or you can simply imagine liberation as freedom from everything that limits your sense of *connessione* to the Divine.)

After making this invocation for yourself, make the same request for your circle of loved ones: "May all those I love be happy. May they be peaceful. May they be free." Then you expand the field of your lovingkindness to include all sentient beings: "May all living things be happy. May they be peaceful. May they be free."

You complete the practice by returning to your initial invocation for yourself, asking, "May I be happy. May I be peaceful. May I be free."

If you like, you can find alternative words that express the same fundamental sentiments, such as: "May I/they be healthy/whole. May I/they be joyful/happy. May I/they be filled with peace/love."

CHAPTER 12

*C*onclusion: *Leonardo's Blessing*

Lao-tzu noted, "Conclusions are ignorance arrested on the path to less ignorance." So, rather than a conclusion, may you find a new beginning as you receive this sevenfold blessing:

> May the spirit of the Maestro's quest touch your personal search for wholeness and truth.
>
> May you find the courage to take full responsibility for your intentions and actions.
>
> May Leonardo's angel inspire you to open your inner eye of perception and savor every moment of existence.
>
> May your darkest places be illuminated by the light of self-acceptance.

May you share with the *Mona Lisa* the deep smile that
emerges from the inner marriage of masculine and feminine.

May your body, emotions, mind, and spirit be integrated
so that you experience boundless energy and vibrant
health.

May your life be filled with beauty, joy, goodness, and
love.

In Leonardo's painting *Adoration of the Magi*, the baby Jesus makes the *mudra* (hand sign)
of Kether. This gesture, which has significance in several spiritual traditions, was not un-
common in Renaissance paintings, and it is repeated in both versions of the *Madonna of
the Rocks*. In the Kabbalah this *mudra* represents the first *sefirah* at the top of the Tree of
Life; in yoga it signifies the crown chakra; and in the Taoist tradition it indicates the realm
of the king of the eastern sky and emperor of the rising sun—the realm where masculine
and feminine energies are one, before yin and yang separate. For Leonardo it was an invocation of the kingdom of heaven, calling down the divine blessing upon us all.

RESOURCES

- If you'd like to support Vebjørn Sand's beautiful vision of a Leonardo Bridge on every continent, please contact Melinda Iverson at brick-fish@msn.com and see the website www.vebjorn-sand.com/the bridge.com.
- Jean Houston's Mystery School offers a unique education in universal wisdom. Contact her at: JeanH@aol.com.
- You can discover more about Byron Katie's remarkable process of spiritual *curiosità* at www.thework.org.
- Gene Jones is the maestro of sound healing. Contact him at www.soundgateways.com.
- For more information about shadow work, contact Dr. Connie Zweig at czweig@aol.com.
- A marvelous resource for balancing male/female energy to promote wholeness and happiness is Lorie Dechar for Five Spirits Acupuncture: www.fivespirits.com.
- Michele Hebert for yoga and meditation retreats: www.spaspirit.com.
- Learn more about Dr. Dale Schusterman's remarkable energy healing work at www.SignLanguageoftheSoul.com.
- The Alexander technique is a simple, profound method for discovering divine proportion in your everyday movement. Contact Michael Frederick at michaeldfrederick@earthlink.net or call 1–800–260–5133.

- Explore Conscious Embodiment with aikido teacher and healer Wendy Palmer, c/o 809 Vendola Drive, San Rafael, CA 94903.
- Experience the *darshan* of pure love with a hug from the Great Mother incarnate: www.amachi.com.
- Discover your life purpose, clarify your goals, and craft a plan to make them real with coaching from Rob Berkley and Debbie Phillips, c/o Rob@groupMV.com.
- To support the application of Leonardo's principles in science education for children please contact: The Discovery Center of Science and Technology, 511 East Third Street, Bethlehem, PA 18015, 1–610–865–5010, ext. 103, ericksonl@discovery-center.org.

APPENDIX: CONVERSATION
WITH THE GRAND MASTER

In the quest to plumb some of the mysteries raised by *The Da Vinci Code*, I consulted with a uniquely qualified code-breaker, Grand Master Raymond Keene, O.B.E.

During World War II, as Britain was fighting for its survival, the nation's intelligence services turned to chess grand masters to help break German codes. Prominent among those who helped crack the vital Enigma code, for example, were former London *Times* chess correspondents Harry Golombek, O.B.E., and Sir Stuart Milner. I asked Grand Master Raymond Keene, O.B.E., their successor at the *Times* (and British chess champion for fourteen years), to help decode some of the ciphers, clues, and codes in *The Da Vinci Code*.

Grand Master Keene responded: "The real da Vinci code has nothing to do with the Priory of Sion, cipher boxes allegedly designed by Leonardo, Opus Dei, Mary Magdalene, or the portrayal of St. John in *The Last Supper*." Keene continues, "In recent reconstructions for BBC Television of Leonardo's aeronautical, military, and aquatic machines it has been uniformly discovered that they seem to go backward and have to be corrected for this before they function. In patronising tones, the reconstructers chide Leonardo: 'You know, well, he was pretty great for the fifteenth century—he got it almost right—you only have to tweak it so the gears go the other way and then of course it works.'

"But," Keene goes on, "they've missed the obvious: the real da Vinci Code! What did they expect from a man who wrote backwards to protect the privacy of his words? Of course the machines are in reverse. This was Leonardo's second layer of encoded defence against unauthorised usage."

Keene observes that the only real codes in Dan Brown's book are anagrams and puns that have very little to do with Leonardo. For example:

- The female protagonist's name, Sophie Neveu, translates as "wisdom nu-eve"—a dual-language pun, with *nu* (French for "naked") in reference to the naked rites Sophie witnesses or, of course, phonetically "new Eve" in English, suggesting a new interpretation of the sacred feminine.
- The protagonist Robert Langdon's name is probably drawn from John Langdon, the renowned ambigrammist (an ambigram is a word reading the same from more than one vantage point, e.g. right side up and upside down).
- The murdered curator, Saunière, is a reference to Béranger Saunière, the abbot of the chapel at Rennes-les-Château, who was the last alleged grand master of the Priory of Sion. Keene observes, "His church is packed with weird symbolism, including a sixty-four-square chessboard engraved into the stone floor of the church that has now become a major tourist attraction."
- Leigh Teabing's name is an anagrammatical conflation of the names Richard Leigh and Michael Baigent, authors of *Holy Blood, Holy Grail,* the book—now enjoying a huge leap in sales—that brought massive attention to the thesis that Mary Magdalene spawned a holy bloodline.
- Detective Fâché's name translates to "angry" in French (which he certainly was through most of the novel—his character represents the anger of the Catholic faithful against the heresies of the Priory).
- The name of Robert Langdon's agent, Faukman, is an anagram for the name of Dan Brown's actual editor, Kaufman.
- On page 392 Brown offers as a clue the pun "We aren't looking for a

Catholic Pope," which eventually points to poet Alexander Pope, who penned these famous lines about the genius of Sir Isaac Newton: "Nature and nature's laws lay hid in night / God said / let Newton be / and all was light!" The only problem with Brown's clue is that both Popes were in fact Catholic!

BIBLIOGRAPHY

Abrams, Jeremiah, and Connie Zweig, editors. *Meeting the Shadow: The Hidden Power of the Dark Side of Human Nature.* Los Angeles: Jeremy P. Tarcher, 1991.

Baigent, Michael, Richard Leigh, and Henry Lincoln. *Holy Blood, Holy Grail.* New York: Bantam Dell, 2004.

Ballentine, Rudolph. *Radical Healing: Integrating the World's Great Therapeutic Traditions to Create a New Transformative Medicine.* New York: Three Rivers Press, 1999.

Barks, Coleman, translator. *The Essential Rumi.* New York: HarperCollins, 1995.

Bennett, J. G. *A Spiritual Psychology.* Gloucestershire, England: Coombe Springs Press, 1974.

———. *Transformation.* Gloucestershire, England: Coombe Springs Press, 1978.

Borysenko, Joan. *The Way of the Mystic: Seven Paths to God.* Carlsbad, CA: Hay House, 1997.

Brown, Dan. *The Da Vinci Code.* New York: Doubleday, 2003.

Bucke, Richard Maurice. *Cosmic Consciousness: A Study in the Evolution of the Human Mind.* New York: Arkana, 1991.

Childre, Doc, and Howard Martin. *The HeartMath Solution.* San Francisco: HarperCollins, 1999.

Chopra, Deepak. *Perfect Health: The Complete Mind/Body Guide*. New York: Harmony Books, 1991.

Clark, Kenneth. *Leonardo da Vinci*. Revised and introduced by Martin Kemp. London: Penguin, 1993.

Coelho, Paulo. *The Alchemist*. San Francisco: HarperSanFrancisco, 1998.

Cohen, Andrew. *An Absolute Relationship to Life*. Lenox, MA: Moksha Foundation, 1997.

Cutler, Howard, and His Holiness the Dalai Lama. *The Art of Happiness*. New York: Penguin Putnam, 1998.

da Vinci, Leonardo. *Leonardo on the Human Body*. Translated and introduced by Charles D. O'Malley and J. B. de C. M. Saunders. New York: Dover, 1983.

———. *The Notebooks of Leonardo da Vinci*. Compiled and edited by Jean Paul Richter. New York: Dover, 1970.

———. *The Notebooks of Leonardo da Vinci*. Edited by Edward MacCurdy. New York: George Brazilier, 1956.

Eisler, Riane. *The Chalice and the Blade: Our History, Our Future*. San Francisco: HarperSanFrancisco, 1988.

Feldman, Daniel Hale. *Qabalah: The Mystical Heritage of the Children of Abraham*. Santa Cruz, CA: Work of the Chariot, 2001.

Gardner, Laurence. *Bloodline of the Holy Grail: The Hidden Lineage of Jesus Revealed*. Gloucester, MA: Fair Winds Press, 2002.

Gelb, Michael J. *How to Think Like Leonardo da Vinci: Seven Steps to Genius Every Day*. New York: Dell, 1998.

Golas, Thaddeus. *The Lazy Man's Guide to Enlightenment*. New York: Bantam, 1980.

Gombrich, E. H. *The Story of Art*. London: Phaidon, 1995.

Katie, Byron. *Loving What Is: Four Questions That Can Change Your Life*. New York: Harmony Books, 2002.

Livio, Mario. *The Golden Ratio: The Story of Phi, the World's Most Astonishing Number*. New York: Broadway Books, 2003.

Marani, Pietro C. *Leonardo da Vinci: The Complete Paintings*. New York: Harry N. Abrams, 2000.

Mitchell, Stephen. *Tao Te Ching*. New York: Harper and Row, 1988.

Moses, Jeffrey. *Oneness: Great Principles Shared by All Religions*. New York: Ballantine, 2002.

Ornstein, Robert. *The Evolution of Consciousness: The Origins of the Way We Think*. New York: Touchstone, 1992.

Otto, Rudolf. *Mysticism East and West: A Comparative Analysis of the Nature of Mysticism*. New York: Macmillan, 1976.

Palmer, Wendy. *The Intuitive Body: Aikido as a Clairsentient Practice*. Berkeley, CA: North Atlantic Books, 1994.

Schimmel, Rosemarie. *The Mystery of Numbers*. New York: Oxford University Press, 1993.

Schusterman, Dale H. *Sign Language of the Soul: A Handbook for Healing*. Cranston, RI: Writers' Collective, 2003.

Shah, Idries. *Wisdom of the Idiots*. New York: E. P. Dutton, 1971.

Suzuki, D. T. *Mysticism: Christian and Buddhist*. New York: Harper and Row, 1971.

Tagore, Rabindranath. *The Collected Poems and Plays*. New York: Collier, 1993.

Vasari, Giorgio. *The Lives of the Artists*. Oxford: Oxford University Press, 1991.

Walsh, Roger. *Essential Spirituality: The Seven Central Practices to Awaken Heart and Mind*. New York: John Wiley & Sons, 1999.

Zukav, Gary. *The Seat of the Soul*. New York: Simon and Schuster, 1990.

Zweig, Connie, and Steve Wolf. *Romancing the Shadow: Illuminating the Dark Side of the Soul*. New York: Ballantine, 1997.

LIST OF ILLUSTRATIONS

CHAPTER 9: CULTIVATE BALANCE *(ARTE/SCIENZA)*
Leonardo da Vinci. *Mona Lisa.* Photo: R. G. Ojeda. Louvre, Paris.
  Photo: Réunion des Musées Nationaux/Art Resource, NY.
Leonardo da Vinci. *Allegories of Ingratitude, envy and death; Pleasure and
  pain.* JBS17. Photo: The Governing Body of Christ Church, Oxford.

CHAPTER 10: NURTURE INTEGRATION *(CORPORALITÀ)*
Leonardo da Vinci. *The Vitruvian Man, ca. 1492.* Accademia, Venice.
  Photo: Scala/Art Resource, NY.
Leonardo da Vinci. *Mechanisms of the Ventricles of the Heart.* The Royal
  Collection copyright © 2004, Her Majesty Queen Elizabeth II.

CHAPTER 11: PRACTICE LOVE *(CONNESSIONE)*
Leonardo da Vinci. *Madonna and Child with Saint Anne and Infant St. John
  the Baptist.* National Gallery, London. Photo: Art Resource, NY.
Leonardo da Vinci. *Adoration of the Magi.* Uffizi, Florence. Photo:
  Alinari/Art Resource, NY.
Leonardo da Vinci. *Adoration of the Magi.* Detail of Christ Child. Uffizi,
  Florence. Photo: Alinari/Art Resource, NY.

ACKNOWLEDGMENTS:
THE SMILE OF LEONARDO

This book project has been touched on many levels by what Jung called "synchronicity." From 1995 to 1997, while researching Leonardo's principles and writing *How to Think Like Leonardo da Vinci*, I spent seven three-week terms in Switzerland codirecting a Renaissance Leadership retreat for the Liechtenstein Global Trust. During this extraordinary series of corporate programs, I was able to develop the presentation of the principles and share ideas with other faculty, including the poet-laureate of Great Britain, Ted Hughes; the chess columnist of the London *Times*, Grand Master Raymond Keene; Renaissance art expert and former director of British intelligence, Sir Brian Tovey; and the originator of mind-mapping, Tony Buzan. The princes of Liechtenstein were able to fund this extraordinary learning experience as part of the expansion of their very successful business partly because twenty years before, they had sold a painting from their remarkable private art collection to the Mellon family, who then donated the work to the National Gallery of Art in Washington, D.C. The painting is the *Portrait of Ginevra de Benci* by Leonardo da Vinci. (I visited the painting many times and sent the princes a postcard with her image and a note saying "Regards from your old friends in D.C.")

Grazie mille to everyone who supported the development of *How to Think Like Leonardo da Vinci*, which in turn led to this book.

In December 2003, while researching this book, I spent a week with the visionary artist Jacqueline Ripstein, who has achieved international acclaim for her luminous, spiritually uplifting imagery. Ripstein's trademarked motto is "If you can see the Invisible, you can do the Impossible." During our time together we shared ideas in her living room, where we had surrounded ourselves with images from many different beautiful illustrated books about Leonardo. As I reached for one of the books, with the intention of leafing through it to find a particular passage from Leonardo's *Treatise on Painting*, I said to Jacqueline, "What we are doing would make Leonardo smile." The instant the words left my mouth we both saw the heading of the page I had randomly opened, which read "The Smile of Leonardo."

Grazie molto to Ripstein and everyone else who has helped bring a smile to Leonardo's face, especially:

Mary Hogan
Joan Gelb
Dr. Sandy Gelb
Jack Ehrlich
Rosa Ehrlich
Molly Gelb
Victor Gelb
J. G. Bennett
Mort Herskowitz, D.O.
Hassan Shushud
Paul Anderson
Naomi Anderson
Professor Martin Kemp
Joan Witkowski
Sir Brian Tovey
Susan Greenberg
Forrest Hainline
Lisa Levy
Linda Carol Strahan
Michelle Hebert
Jean Houston, Ph.D.
Jill Baron, M.D.
Melinda Iverson

Vebjørn Sand
Grand Master Raymond Keene
Connie Zweig, Ph.D.
Mona Lisa Schulz, M.D., Ph.D.
Penny Levin
Marvin Hyett, M.D.
Jennifer Spoelker
Jeannie Becker
Rob Berkley
Taya Levine
Jook Leung

Grazie mille to those who made very special contributions to this book:

Esther Cohen
Leslie Copland
Dr. Dale Schusterman
Lorie Dechar

And *grazie mille* to all at Bantam Dell who have supported this book, especially Irwyn Applebaum, the publisher; Ellen Cipriano, who created the design; Glen Edelstein, who oversaw it; Jorge Martínez, who created the jacket; my wonderful editor, Beth Rashbaum, and her assistant, Melissa Pimentel. *Grazie mille* also to Muriel Nellis and Jane Roberts of Literary and Creative Artists, who inspired more smiles when, in finalizing the details of the agreement with Beth Rashbaum for the delivery of this manuscript, agreed on a due date of April 15—which just happens to be Leonardo's birthday.

ABOUT THE AUTHOR

Michael J. Gelb is a globally acclaimed pioneer in the fields of accelerated learning, creative thinking, and leadership development. He is the president of High Performance Learning, an international management training and consulting firm based in the New York metropolitan area. Established in 1977, HPL's clients include BP, Du Pont, KPMG, Merck, Microsoft, Nike, and Western Union. Michael Gelb is the author of the *New York Times* business best-seller *How to Think Like Leonardo da Vinci*, which has been translated into eighteen languages. Gelb is also the author of *The New Mind Map, Present Yourself: Captivate Your Audience with Great Presentations, Thinking for a Change,* and *Discover Your Genius: How to Think Like History's Ten Most Revolutionary Minds*. A fourth-degree black belt in the martial art of aikido, Gelb is coauthor with chess grand master Raymond Keene of *Samurai Chess: Mastering Strategy Through the Martial Art of the Mind*. Michael Gelb's first book, *BodyLearning: An Introduction to the Alexander Technique,* debuted in 1981 and has become the standard text in the field.

Michael Gelb's work has been featured in the *New York Times*, the *London Review of Books, Executive Excellence,* the *Washington Post, USA Today, Investor's Business Daily, Industry Week,* and many other publications. A former professional juggler, Gelb has juggled live on *Good Morning America* and appeared onstage with Mick Jagger and the

Rolling Stones and Bob Dylan. Gelb is also the author of *More Balls Than Hands: Juggling Your Way to Success by Learning to Love Your Mistakes.*

In 1999, Gelb was the co-recipient, with former senator John Glenn, of the Brain Foundation Brain-of-the-Year Award (previous winners include Stephen Hawking, Bill Gates, Garry Kasparov, and Gene Roddenberry). In 2002, Gelb received a Batten Fellowship, awarded by the University of Virginia's Darden Graduate School of Business. He lives in Edgewater, New Jersey.